WHEN THE
Holy Spirit
CALLS

Embracing Your Unique Spiritual Gifts

TILICIA L. MAYO - GAMBLE

Disclaimer:

To protect the privacy of certain individuals, their names have been changed.

"Behold, I stand at the door, and knock: if any man hear my voice, and open the door, I will come in to him, and will sup with him, and he with me."
(Revelations 3:20, KJV)

Acknowledgments

This book is the work of the Holy Spirit speaking through me. Around the time He inspired me to write this book, a gentleman by the name of Elder Hugh Hall told me that the Lord had given me an assignment and that I did not have a choice. I must be obedient. This was the confirmation I needed to trust that the Lord had indeed instructed me to write this book. By being obedient, I hope the Lord is well pleased. I would like to acknowledge Monica Dilworth for encouraging me to move forward with writing this book during the low times when I questioned if this was the Lord's will and feared what those around me would say or how they would respond. You reassured me that any handiwork created to glorify the Lord and edify His people would be pleasing in His sight. I also want to acknowledge my husband, Johnny Gamble. Even when you don't understand my relationship with the Holy Spirit or the things He reveals to me, it has never stopped you from encouraging me to stay strong in my faith or to follow God's path for my life. When the Lord offers us a word of revelation, sometimes it takes another God-breathed soul to affirm the message. For me, this person was Evelyn Chavers. When I shared a passage from the very early stages of this book, she said, "Well, He gave it to you just as He wanted you to say it." To the Agape Worship Center Women's Ministry for showing me that writing can be a spiritual gift. I am the scribe, but my Heavenly Father is the author. To my family and my friends, I pray that by reading this book, you will come to know me in the way God sees me. And finally, I'd like to acknowledge Cherry Littles, who encouraged me not to worry about whether I was writing a good book and to allow the eyes of my heart to be enlightened. You told me that this was not my book at all, but that it is God's book. Indeed, it is.

Table Of Contents

Introduction — Ask, Seek, Knock

"Ask and it will be given to you; seek and you will find; knock and the door will be opened to you. For everyone who asks receives; he who seeks finds; and to him who knocks, the door will be opened. (Matthew 7:7-8, NIV)

I had no intention of writing a memoir on my spiritual journey. When I began to hear the Lord's voice, I found myself in a state of fear and confusion, without a spiritual guide or the biblical foundation to help me understand what I was experiencing. As a child, I was raised to go to church, but I would not say that I was raised in the church, nor did I grow up learning about spiritual gifts. Needless to say, I had no grasp of charisma or the operation of the Holy Spirit. Yet, there I was, growing spiritually. When I began serving in the church and putting God's work above my personal desires, all that began to change. The Lord began calling me, inviting me to have intimacy with the Holy Spirit, but I didn't know how to answer.

There came a time in my spiritual journey when the next steps were clear. I was practicing a discipline of

1

devotion: reading my Bible daily, attending Bible study, listening to sermons, and praying consistently throughout the day. The challenge was that I did not realize spending time with the Holy Spirit meant cultivating a relationship. It was the key to creating a space for God to share all He wanted me to know. But, if I knew then what I know now, I would have sought spiritual guidance before seeking to establish a relationship with the Lord! I wish someone had told me that once I sought the Lord, when I began speaking with the Holy Spirit, I should be prepared to listen because, without a doubt, He would speak back. He provided instruction, and as I began to heed that instruction, the Holy Spirit began to remove the veil and reveal hidden truths. He invited me into His spiritual domain, which took me further and further away from this earthly physical world. While I knew many Christians long for the day when the Lord would reveal His Spirit realm to them, this experience frightened me. How do you share this experience with others without being judged? Without being told that your feelings and experiences are not normal? I soon learned that without the prayers and support of spiritually-minded people to support you, you could find yourself allowing fear to take over or even retreating, telling God that you don't want His spiritual gifts.

Furthermore, you keep the Good News of God's grace to yourself. This is a lonely place, a lonely feeling. It can become a burden that is too heavy to carry alone.

This burden was one that I carried out of fear that others would not believe me, that others would judge or criticize me. I feared that I would judge myself for not getting it right, for not knowing enough, or that I did not sound the way my church leaders sounded. Even more frightening than not believing, was believing. The Holy Spirit had begun to show me inconceivable things, or at least things I thought impossible. I thought, *"What do I do with this?"*

To accept a calling from the Holy Spirit means believing in things that cannot be explained in this world. The term "supernatural," while understated, perfectly describes the manifestation of the Holy Spirit and believing that... the Lord would use ME, of all people, to experience and witness the stirring up that could only be the result of....well, GOD. I soon learned that I was not the only person who feared how God was using me. It was those in my inner circle who helped me to remember that the Lord said, *"...do not fear, for I am with you; do not be dismayed, for I am your God. I will strengthen you and help you."* (Isaiah 41:10). We must all learn and accept that we are chosen. We must embrace the Holy Spirit's invitation and answer His call. As you read this book, I want you to know how the Lord sees you through His eyes and through the eyes of others. You are His handiwork, created to do good works.

If you have ever received a prophecy or discerned a spirit, and it made you uncomfortable or fearful, you are not alone. By reading this book, you will walk with me as I take you on my spiritual journey into intimacy with the Holy Spirit. It's a journey of being used by the Holy Spirit, even when I didn't know what that meant. I will take you through my personal encounters with the Holy Spirit, my emotional responses, and the *great cloud of witnesses* that kept me from fleeing from the gifts of the Holy Spirit so that I could live out His calling and His purpose for my life. These witnesses are my spiritual support system. Individuals who experienced the same fears when the Holy Spirit began manifesting His power through them supernaturally. Finally, I will guide you through my ultimate submission to being used in the ways He seeks to use me.

I wrote this book recognizing that there will be many unbelievers, people who will challenge these experiences. I wrote it knowing that there will be people who have never received a revelation that caused them to be fearful. Yet, I am reminded of Paul's message to the Corinthians, *"11God knows we are sincere, and I hope you know this, too. 12Are we commending ourselves to you again? No, we are giving you a reason to be proud of us, so you can answer those who brag about having a spectacular ministry rather than having a sincere heart. [13]If it seems we are crazy, it is to bring glory to God. And if we are in our right minds, it is for your benefit."* (2 Corinthians 5:11-13, NLT). For those of you who have been called by the Lord and are seeking reassurance, I have a responsibility to *bear witness to the good news of God's grace.* If you are willing to take the Holy Spirit's hand, He will equip you with the provisions you need to overcome fear, take your rightful place as His servant and edify His people. This book is for anyone who hears Him but doesn't know how to answer… *When the Holy Spirit Calls.*

Chapter 1:
Stepping Out

In the last days, God says, I will pour out my Spirit on all people. Your sons and daughters will prophesy, your young men will see visions, your old men will dream dreams. (Acts 2:17, NIV)

Receiving the Spirit baptism was a pivotal moment in my intimacy with the Holy Spirit. It was the moment that unlocked the door that would allow the Spirit to pour into me and begin to operate through me, showing me His hidden truths. In this book, I will share with you the events that occurred in the development of my intimate relationship with the Holy Spirit. Perhaps development is not the right word. When I reflect on the years throughout my life, the presence of the Holy Spirit was always there. I sensed Him. But it was only in recent years that the Holy Spirit began to manifest His power through me, allowing me to deepen my relationship with Him. Like any relationship you cultivate, spend time in, and seek out, I developed not only a relationship with the Holy Spirit but an intimacy with the Holy Spirit.

Water baptism is one form of baptism. There is another type, the *baptism of the Holy Spirit* (Luke 3:16). In

Christianity, a well-discussed assertion is that the evidence of spiritual baptism is the gift of tongues, known as speaking in tongues.

All of them were filled with the Holy Spirit and began to speak in other tongues as the Spirit enabled them. (Acts 2:4, NIV).

By no means does this devalue the importance of the other spiritual gifts. This notion of the evidence of spiritual baptism comes from Acts 2:4 when the Holy Spirit came upon the disciples for the first time and caused them to speak in tongues. But how does someone know when they have experienced the Spirit baptism if there is no evidence of speaking in tongues? I still have never spoken in tongues. So, does that mean that I have not truly received a spiritual baptism? No. I truly believe that I have been baptized in the Holy Spirit.

Many churches have a weekly prayer line or prayer call. It's a way for members to fellowship with one another via phone (or virtually), request prayer, submit a prayer, or even hear church announcements. I worked with the mother of my church to start a prayer line during the COVID-19 pandemic. It was a time when prayer was needed and a time for us to stay connected with church members. My role on the call was, and still is, to oversee and facilitate. I read scriptures aloud, and I pray during the call. One night, while praying, the words flowed in a way I had never experienced. The words flowed through me without my knowledge, control, or thoughts. That was the moment my relationship with the Holy Spirit changed. At this moment, I stepped outside my body and watched myself pray. I, like the women on the call, received prayer rather than being the person who prayed. The Holy Spirit, who had resided in me all this time, had interceded. The Apostle Paul had a perfect description for this moment, *"Whether it was in the body or out of the body I do not know—God knows."* (2 Corinthians 12:2, NIV).

While Paul describes this as paradise, for me, the moment was frightening. *"What just happened?"* I thought. In the days after, I began to feel and sense everything. I had a heightened sense of the Holy Spirit's presence. From that point, my knowledge of the Holy Spirit changed. Before, I knew Him from what the Bible tells me about Him, what Christianity had taught me about Him. Now, I know Him because I have experienced Him. When we experience fear, our brain responds. It tells us to fight, flee, freeze, or fawn. While natural, these are not appropriate responses to the calling of the Holy Spirit. These are our fleshly responses. Things of the Spirit, however, require a spiritual response, a response of faith, a response of submission. To do this, I had to surround myself with other "spirit-filled" individuals (spiritual advisors). I needed spiritual guidance, and I needed to invite the Holy Spirit into my life as a teacher. Without these, I would have been tempted to flee---to flee against encounters that my mind told me were not real, things that we are told do not exist. Only then could I accept that the Holy Spirit was trying to complete His works through me.

You're Covered

When I was 23, I made the decision to be water baptized. There was not a particular event or circumstance that prompted my decision to be baptized. I had not previously made the decision to be baptized, and that sat on my heart. As the pastor asked if there were any candidates for baptism, this felt like an act that every Christian should take and one that, until then, I neglected to do. I'm not sure what the process of making this decision looks like as a child. When I made the decision as an adult, it felt like an important step in my relationship with God. I recall asking my mom about it as a child. She felt that it was important to make this decision, but only when you fully understood the meaning. I won't argue the benefits of receiving water baptism as a child versus an adult. As long as this important declaration of your commitment to the Lord is made, it is the right decision. I once heard that when you are baptized, the Lord sends you a message. For me, that message was, "You're covered." Because of Jesus' sacrifice, long before I was ever a thought, I was covered (Psalm 91). The difference was, now I knew it.

The message of being covered was not immediately apparent. I did not come out of the water with a newfound sense that the Lord had covered me. However, it did not take long, a week, days even. One night, I was working late. I had to attend a community meeting. When the meeting ended, it was dark, and I was not parked nearby. Before I walked out, one of my colleagues stopped me. He was a male colleague. He turned to me and asked, "Are you afraid?" I expressed to him that it was not the safest neighborhood, and it was dark outside. He then asked, "Do you believe in the blood of Jesus Christ and that He died for your sins?" I believed and told him so. At that point, he said to me that not only should I not fear walking to my car but that I, specifically, would never have to fear any circumstances such as these because *I was covered*. Not only did this resonate with me, but it felt familiar. It felt like an anointing that had already existed over my life.

Prevenient grace, or enabling grace, is a grace that precedes human action or decisions. It reflects God's heart for you and is His way of showing love to you at any point. In its simplest terms, God shows His love for you and works on your behalf long before you are aware of it. It has been described that prevenient grace is the work of the Holy Spirit drawing us to God.[1] The Holy Spirit knew long before my baptism that I was His (Jeremiah 1:5). However, it can take some of us a lifetime to realize this. While I was not raised in the church, soon

---

[1] Tony Richie. (2022). *Essentials of Pentecostal Theology.*

after my birth, my mother dedicated me back to the Lord. As she puts it, she did not understand the process in great detail, but she knew that if her children were to follow the Lord's will and be covered by His blood, she wanted to make a public declaration. Perhaps this was the draw, the call, or maybe it's the reason I was able to hear the call. From that moment, I no longer felt that I was just another name in the Book of the Lamb. I had become the image He had imagined, placed in this physical world to worship and to be of service.

Journey into an Unknown Land

In 2017, my husband and I moved to southern Georgia. I did not realize it at the time, but this move would be a pivotal moment in my life. This part of Georgia is a very rural area, much different from where I grew up. I was born and raised in Gary, Indiana, a small urban city in the Midwest. Moving to Georgia felt like I was on foreign soil. The culture was very different. It was a constant reminder of how far I was from home. I had no family in Georgia. We had family in neighboring states, which helped, but I felt so far away from my loved ones. I moved to Georgia after accepting a position as a professor at the local university. However, I was not remotely interested in staying in Georgia. I prayed over the decision to accept the job offer. When my husband and I visited, he asked me, "Are you sure you want to come here?" I wasn't sure at all. I felt confident about one thing: God had led me to this place.

When I felt God had spoken about my move to Georgia, I did not hesitate. I was anxious; I did not know anything about living in the South, and I had never once visited a rural area, but I was obedient. This move helped me to understand that when the Lord asks you to move to an unknown land or unfamiliar territory, you move without hesitation, having faith that the provision for such a destination will await your arrival. There are many examples in the Bible of God's command to leave a place of comfort. Following my move, I was reminded of God's command of Abram.

The Lord had said to Abram, "Go from your country, your people, and your father's household to the land I will show you." (Genesis 12:1, NIV).

There were many times when I was completely surrounded by people, some I did not know, some I had come to know, but I could not call any of them family. For that reason, I felt a sense of loneliness.

The land where I walked was completely unfamiliar. To see my family, I would have to drive 12-14 hours by car or take a 4-hour flight and then drive an additional 2 hours. There were no direct flights, so my husband and I often drove instead of spending a day flying and sitting in airports. Transportation was not the real issue. I missed my homeland, I missed my family, and yet, my Father had instructed me to be here for His service. I received inspirational messages during this time that helped me get through. Messages such as, "When God wants to do a great work in you, oftentimes He will isolate you, remove you from your place of comfort." I heard that I should "embrace the times when God sets me apart." These messages did not heal my feelings or emotions, but they gave me hope. The move was an easy act of obedience. Staying was the hard part.

The Prophetess

In March 2020, just around the time the COVID pandemic hit the U.S., my church had a revival. The revival concluded with a prophetess. During that time, I had been frustrated with God. I was a few years into my tenure-track faculty position, and it had become quite apparent that the Lord had given me a gift to help and encourage others, to lead them to success. Yet, it did not feel as though I was a recipient of this gift. During the revival, the speaker (the prophetess) said things that truly expressed how I felt at times—*that your gift is working to help others succeed, but you feel left out or left behind.* She said that it was not the devil that put you in a hard place; it was God. She said that sometimes you don't want the gift God gave you because it's draining and it hurts you, but it helps others. These comments not only resonated with me, but they also embodied everything I had been feeling at the time. She wasn't speaking to me directly, but for the first time in a long time, I felt seen.

My purpose for discussing this experience is to convey my thoughts, at the time at least, on the gift of prophecy. This woman referred to herself as a prophetess. It was and still is not my place to judge. At the time, I did not know how to feel about those who referred to themselves with the title of prophet or prophetess. I was taught that these are not words that one needs to use to describe themselves, that others would see and affirm that the Holy Spirit is operating within them through the gift of prophecy. More important, the Lord anoints people to these roles. When I attended this revival, I didn't know if the gift of prophecy or any other charismatic gift was real. I was doubtful. Not everyone grows up knowing or believing that prophecy is real. There are those (traditionalists) who believe that the gifts of the Spirit do not exist for us today the way they did in biblical days and that we have no use for them today. Fast forward two years later, and the joke (so to speak) was on me.

The Lord had taken me on a spiritual journey from skepticism to experience to….belief. I had judged others for acknowledging the power of the spiritual gifts only to begin experiencing them myself. I wrestled with feeling cynical but also fearful. There were times when God confirmed that He had spoken to me, that He guided me, and told me not only who to pray for, but what to pray for...and that scared me. I was frightened by the idea of knowing what to pray for someone when you have never had a conversation with that person. I was frightened by the visions of them when they were not in my presence, receiving revelation. Just the thought of these experiences makes me pause, overcome with emotion, being taken back to those moments. I feared the physical feeling I experienced and the lack of control I felt over my body. I feared that the people I approached would think that I was lying or being dishonest. At the time, what I feared most was that it was not real and that it was all in my head. Am I crazy? Am I imagining things? Am I hallucinating? This would make sense. The things I had experienced were irrational and the best way for me to rationalize this was to say that it was all in my head.

Chapter 2:
Operating In The Spirit Realm

Now to each one the manifestation of the Spirit is for the common good...All these are the work of one and the same Spirit, and he distributes them to each one, just as he determines (1 Corinthians 12:7,11 NIV).

Hearing His Voice

A few years ago, my sister and I began practicing Daniel's fast. Each year, we start the year off with a fast. Since then, I've developed a discipline of consistent prayer, modeled after Daniel, praying at least three intentional times per day. One of my prayer sessions occurs during the middle of the day at 2:00 p.m. I stop whatever I'm doing for a moment of intentional prayer. Sometimes, this is a quiet moment to allow the Lord to speak to me if He desires to do so. I want to make sure I can hear Him. At one point, due to the busyness of my schedule, I got off track. Since I did not have the time to sit and be thoughtful in my prayer time, I figured it was disrespectful to pause for a few seconds of prayer. The

Lord deserved more. He deserved more of my time and more of my attention. If I could not give Him that space, then I needed to wait to pray. I thought, *"The Lord is not pleased with how I'm praying."* So, I stopped praying in the midday.

One night, I called a friend from church, Ms. Cherry. She is one of my three spirit-filled confidantes. She has been with the church since its inception and has brought innumerable souls to salvation. When I first met Ms. Cherry, it was a women's meeting. She sat down next to me and quickly introduced herself. I thought that she was very outgoing, quite the opposite of how I perceive myself. I did not say much to her then, but now she has become someone from whom I seek spiritual guidance. I explained to Ms. Cherry a dream I had been having, a dream that did not quite feel like a dream. Someone had been calling my name at night, waking me out of my sleep. I didn't think it was real. Another night, again, I heard someone calling out to me. But this time, it was my mother's voice. Once again, I thought that I was dreaming. After I did not respond to the voices, I was then awakened by the sound of someone beating at the front door. No one was there. My husband did not hear anything. "How could he not?" I wondered. Ms. Cherry told me that I was not dreaming and that what I was experiencing was the Lord calling me. I thought that she misunderstood me. She told me that I should wake up at the same time the Lord had been calling me and that I should pray. And so, I did. I woke up, and I went to the Lord.

Instead of speaking as I normally do for prayer, I invited Him to speak to me.

> *Speak, for your servant is listening.*
> *(1 Samuel 3:10, NIV)*

And then it happened quite vividly; there were flashes of "2:00" surrounding me. All around me were flashes of clocks at the 2:00 hour. With a voice of conviction, the Lord expressed His disappointment. It was the voice of a parent, a Father. It was no wonder that He had used my mother's voice to try to get my attention. He missed talking with me, and He wanted our time back. Was it just the result of my active imagination? Or was Ms. Cherry right? I wasn't sure. But at the time, I simply prayed that it was real. I responded by asking the Lord for forgiveness, and I told Him, "I hear you, Lord. I'm here."

Several weeks later, the pastor of my church spoke about hearing God's voice. He explained that when the Lord speaks to you, He will speak with the voice of someone in an authoritative role in your life (e.g., a parent or a teacher). The pastor used Samuel as an example of hearing from the Lord. Samuel thought he was hearing Eli, but as it turned out, Samuel was hearing directly from God. The story of Samuel has further meaning in my life. (I will discuss the similarities of Samuel in a later chapter.) But this confirmed why I had heard the Lord in the way that I did. When I did not respond, He used the voice of one of my parents. Do you know that feeling of being "special" when you realize someone wants to talk to you? That they are interested in what you have to say? To know that in this case, it was the Lord, was a humbling experience that I cannot put into words, nor can I describe on paper. Our Heavenly Father has billions of children on this earth, and yet, He wanted to hear what I had to say.

I met with a church leader, Bishop Anthony Chavers, to discuss all I had been experiencing. The Bishop, as I call him, founded the church I attend. People often characterize him as being a prophet. I had never heard him refer to himself as a prophet, but I was aware of his gift of bringing a prophetic word to others. The Bishop has a degree in theology and often connects with those who appreciate education. As a professor and researcher by trade, people are quick to characterize me as an intellectual but often neglect to pause to consider the fullness of my character. They often will not hear me witness my interpretation of how the Holy Spirit uses my position in the classroom to reach His sheep. The Bishop understood that I could be both an intellectual and someone with a heightened spiritual sensitivity and that I am expressive about my role in the kingdom of the Most High God.

Before meeting with the Bishop, I had a brief conversation with a career coach. During the discussion, the coach asked me what I planned to do about moving into the role where God was trying to place me. To her surprise, I answered quite firmly, "I do not know." Within the next hour, I arrived at a coffee shop, and sitting there was the Bishop. He was reading a book, *Essentials of Pentecostal Theology*, by Tony Richie. The Bishop recommended that I read the book. At that moment, it felt like reading the book would be the first step to walking into whatever God was calling me to.

In my follow-up discussions with the Bishop, I was finally able to be vulnerable and share my encounters with the Holy Spirit. Things I had never said to anyone. He was accepting of what I had to say. More importantly, he acknowledged that

> *Is it real? What is It? No one will believe me. Who is she that God would use her?*

my fear was normal. I knew that the Lord spoke to me, but my clarity, my inner peace, was with the presence of the Holy Spirit. Saying those words aloud made me overcome with emotion. It is clear to me when angels have been in my presence. The scripture says that we have entertained angels unawares. I believed that it was possible to know when they have been in your presence. What does that mean? Why does God allow us to sense when His angels are present?

I did not understand all the spiritual gifts. In fact, the concept of "spiritual gifts" was quite new to me, but I knew that God had blessed me with spiritual gifts and had begun the process of awakening them within me. The fear that the Bishop talked about fell into two categories: a fear of God using me in a way that would be so powerful that it scared me, and the fear of people thinking that I was, for lack of a better word, "crazy." I knew that the Lord had called out to me, but how do you explain that to others? Is it real? What is it? Will anyone believe me? Who is she that God would use her in that way? While I had so many questions, they were not getting me anywhere. I was asking the wrong questions.

For me, it was unclear what my spiritual gifts were. I could only describe how the Holy Spirit was using me. I can discern when the Lord gives me an assignment. When I am tasked with giving someone a word or a message, I can recall Bible scripture with full clarity. Yet, when I try to recite Bible verses in my own desire, I cannot seem to recall verses well. This helped me understand the difference between my knowledge and memory versus the Holy Spirit using me. The Holy Spirit is there to guide me. The challenge was He was using me in a way that was so powerful that a (big) part of me just wanted to say, "No, Lord, choose someone else." Yet, there was a small part of me which understood that by not embracing what He had placed inside of me, I was interfering with God's will.

Levels To Operating in The Spirit

> *"Call to me and I will answer you and tell you
> great and unsearchable things you do not know."*
> (Jeremiah 33:3 NIV)

What I appreciate the most about meeting with the Bishop is that he believed me. Walking around with what felt like a secret, something I felt that I could not express to others out of fear of how they would respond, was a bitter pill to swallow. I felt I had a safe space to share my encounters with the Holy Spirit and learn how to allow the Holy Spirit to use me for His service. To my surprise, the Bishop shared that he, too, feared his spiritual giftings when he first received them. Out of his experience, the Bishop cautioned me not to retreat. Turning away from the gifts of the Holy Spirit and asking Him to take them back was like receiving an invitation from the Lord and sending it back circled, "No, thank you," or receiving a call from the Lord and hitting the decline button. The Bishop warned me, "Dr. Gamble (as he calls me) when you don't appreciate the gifts, the Lord will take them back." When we don't appreciate the gifts of the Holy Spirit, in a sense, we are rejecting His gifts. While I did not want the Lord to take away this opportunity, this occasion, accepting it, was easier said than done.

The Bishop gave me several recommendations to help me overcome my fear of embracing spiritual gifts. First, he told me to read books by Fuchsia Pickett. He wanted me to understand that there are levels to this. He did not explain what "this" was. Thinking back, it was good for me that he did not define it. At that moment, if he had labeled it or named a specific gift, I certainly would have leaned to my own understanding or even to his knowledge rather than focusing on the revelation from the Lord. The Bishop also gave me the names of two individuals with whom I could speak to help me through my new level of spiritual growth. One of them was his mother, Evelyn Chavers. He informed me that she, too, experienced fear when the Holy Spirit began to use her. What struck me the most is that the Bishop said that He identified only one other person in his life who had expressed their profound connection to the Holy Spirit in the way I described—Mother Evelyn.

Mother Evelyn and I had already developed a close spiritual bond. I was comfortable speaking with her about my spiritual journey. At the time, I felt that if I was going to embrace my spiritual gifts, I just needed to get them out in the open. I needed to say it aloud. I needed to tell people! Somehow, I thought this would help me get through all my emotions. Most of all, I was concerned about telling Mom or my family members about how the Lord speaks to me and through me. Mother Evelyn said that I would not need to. She said that I shouldn't. When the Lord was ready, people would see, and then they would know. She also advised me to be obedient. If the Lord gives you a word for someone, speak it. If He sends you to someone to encourage them, then encourage them. It was just that simple. Through this obedience, we can move through the fear and allow the Holy Spirit to flow His power through us.

I cannot underscore enough the value of obedience. You can be fearful; that's ok, but you MUST obey God's instruction. If God perceives that you will not use the provision of spiritual gifts to edify His people, then it sends a message that He cannot use you. The sacrifice of walking up to strangers with a message from the Lord is my way of saying, "I give myself to you so you can use me." Imagine what the Lord has to offer when He realizes He can trust you. He authorizes you and gives you the authority to operate in His power. It is your obedience that signals God to unlock the door to greater levels of intimacy with the Holy Spirit. Through this intimacy, the Holy Spirit unveils hidden truths that will allow you to serve Him in ways that you could not imagine were possible.

It was a couple of months before the Lord would instruct me to deliver a message at the moment of receiving it. I traveled back to my childhood home in Indiana. I was visiting my mother after she had a hard time leading up to Mother's Day. My grandmother's birthday was around Mother's Day. She had passed about nine years prior, but for those of you who have lost a mother, you know that the grief never truly goes away.

While visiting, my husband and I attended my mother's church, and there was a teenage girl, Amber, sitting in front of me. I thought about the things I was supposed to say to her. I could see this young girl in an image engrained in my thoughts, yet I had never met her. But it was just like I'd imagined myself speaking to others time and time again. So, how could I know if this was really the Lord speaking to me to offer encouragement to this young girl? For this reason, I asked the Lord for a sign that the message was coming from Him and not from me. Then Amber "accidentally" bumped my arm, and I looked at her. The Lord told me that if I could not tell if it was the Holy Spirit or me, I should pray with her. I had prayed with or for countless others. I know for sure that when I pray, the Holy Spirit is present. I knew that through prayer, the Holy Spirit would not allow me to say things that were not coming from Him. And so, I did. I prayed.

I asked Amber's Mom, Karyn, if I could pray with her daughter. I also asked Karyn to pray with us. My Mom joined us as well. Immediately, Karyn began to cry. She asked my Mom how I could know what was going on with her daughter. I couldn't. I didn't know. I only said what the Holy Spirit asked me to say. Karyn said that she felt something come over her and that she was in a state of unbelief. She told me that she knew the Lord had spoken to me because there was no way that I could have known that the things I spoke were what she had been telling her daughter. She felt that, as a parent, she was not getting through to Amber. I believe the Lord wanted someone other than her parents to offer her guidance.

I could visualize myself having this conversation with Amber. What troubled me was that I had previously envisioned the Lord speaking through me on so many occasions. I thought it was my imagination. Was this His way of sending me a word for those I had come into contact with? If so, how long had I missed the call for me to speak on His behalf? That day, I felt that I had been obedient to what the Lord had instructed me to do. The young girl's Mom was filled with the Holy Spirit. She knew indeed that she could not deny the presence of the Holy Spirit. I thank God for using me in this way. It's like Fuchsia Pickett said in one of her books, *Walking in the Anointing of the Holy Spirit*[2], that the Holy Spirit will bring a prophecy to someone who is not a prophet.

The other amazing part of this experience was that my mother was present. Not only did Amber's Mom pray with us, but my mother prayed with us. That means she witnessed. It was just like Mother Evelyn had described. I did not have to say anything; my mother just knew. She said that I had blessed Karyn by praying with them. Karyn had almost given up on church because they had

---

[2] Fuchsia Pickett, 2004, Walking in the Anointing of the Holy Spirit, Charisma House.

been having a hard time. Amber said that she loves God and that she did not understand why her friends did not. She was thirteen years old, and the other children in school made fun of her. The Lord wanted her to know that He had set her apart. He wanted her to know that there would come a day when people would call her blessed. That she has been called, not for a time such as this, but for an appointed time. Setting her apart now was His way of preparing her to serve Him in the future. Praise God. Praise God that He would send someone a message in their time of need. Praise the Holy Spirit that He would use me to do it. And praise the Lord that I would be a witness to Him blessing others. This was not me. This was the Holy Spirit. My presence was as a spectator. I watched. I listened. My lips moved. But the Spirit spoke.

The other person the Bishop referred me to was Dr. Enola Mosley. She attended my church and sought out the Bishop when she began to experience the gifts of the Holy Spirit. Dr. Enola has also been a member of the church since it began. I consider her to be one of my three confidantes. Ironically, she considers me to be her mentor. As it turns out, Dr. Enola and I have a great deal in common as it relates to our connection with the Holy Spirit. I began to speak with her about my past frustrations with the Lord. Oftentimes, the Lord sends me to people just before they transition from this world. It causes me a great deal of pain to catch up or to be introduced to someone, and then suddenly, they are gone, leaving me to grieve. It seems that the Holy Spirit uses me to bring peace to His children before they transition to their final resting place. During this transition, His saints may be seeking to find peace, to find rest.

Dr. Enola suggested that she has never known anyone to be used by the Lord the way He uses me to bring peace to those preparing to transition. She said that He does it because I am pure in heart. No one had ever said that to me before. I also was not sure that I was worthy of such a compliment. Psalm 116:15 says, *"Precious in the sight of the Lord is the death of his faithful saints."* I understand the gravity of the death of the saints in God's eyes. So, I am embracing the gift of being with His saints and helping them as they transition to be with our Father in His heavenly kingdom. This moment, while challenging, is not designed for me to be hurt or sad. The moment is not about me but for those who need to be comforted by the thought that while death is imminent, it is not the end. Quite the contrary, it is the beginning.

Minister Penny Gary- Minister Gary was a woman who joined our church's prayer line during the pandemic. She was a member of a different church in town. Meeting through their profession, Minister Gary and Dr. Enola were friends, best friends. Minister Gary was a minister, a teacher, and a true woman of God. For most of her life, Minister Gary taught accounting and other business courses to high school students, but importantly, she was a mentor. She left an indelible mark on her students. I never had the pleasure of meeting Minister Gary in person, but I was drawn to her. One day, during my midday prayer time, I asked the Holy Spirit a question I typically ask during the day, "Holy Spirit, what do you want me to do? Who do you want me to reach out to? What do you want me to say?" On this day, the Holy Spirit instructed me to call Minister Gary. What do you do when He offers His instruction to you? You do what He tells you. That's exactly what I did.

That evening, I called Minister Gary. My cell phone number was not local, so I did not expect her to answer. At first, she did not answer, but she called back. I introduced myself, but she recognized my voice immediately. She was incredibly grateful. Minister Gary told me that I had given her something she had asked the Lord for—someone who was unrelated to her to care enough to call and check in on her. As a schoolteacher, Minister Gary answered countless calls from students during their times of need. She wanted someone to do the same for her. As we ended our call, she thanked me for my obedience.

A few months later, I began the prayer call by reading a poem, "Tomorrow" by Edgar Albert Guest.[3] I like to switch things up from time to time (e.g., song lyrics, poems, devotional readings), but it depends on the Holy Spirit's leading. Minister Gary reacted to the poem by stating it confirmed that she had done the right thing the night before. She always left her phone on to help her students. The previous night, Minister Gary did not want to answer her phone, but she decided to answer it anyway. She was being obedient. What she did not know was that very soon, she would not see tomorrow. We think that God's purpose for us is so grandiose, but the truth is, sometimes He just wants you to pick up the phone, answer a call, or, in my case, make a phone call. Minister Gary told us she knew that when the time came for the Lord to take her, she would not be leaving a "tomorrow" list. She had fulfilled God's purpose for her life. Minister Gary made her transition to be with our Heavenly Father the following week.

It was God's will that my introduction to Minister Gary occurred at the end of her life on this earth. Holy Spirit led me to call her, and He led me to read the poem. My last interactions with Minister Gary allowed me to witness peace and contentment in a person's life before transitioning home to be with our Heavenly Father. Yet, I

---

[3] Collected Works of Edgar Guest" Cutchogue, NY: Buccaneer Books, p. 72

was conflicted. I saw the beauty in her transition, but I also mourned for the person with whom I had developed a brief spiritual connection. I wondered why He would bring me to her only to take her away. But that was the wrong perspective. It wasn't about me. It was about the love between a Father and a daughter. He was calling her home. I was just there to see her off. It was not the first nor the last time the Lord would call me to be there for someone's last days in this physical world.

Mother Phillips- Mother Phillips was a woman from church and a member of the Mothers' Board. I never personally met Mother Phillips when she was able to attend church. I was introduced to her through the prayer line. Mother Phillips joined us from time to time. I looked forward to her calls because she always had a song in her heart. For about 60 seconds, she would sing to her heart's content. When I had not heard from her in a while, I gave her a call. Those calls were consistent over the next two years. During the COVID pandemic, Mother Phillips began a decline from heart failure. She was unable to leave her home, which made our calls much sweeter. In Spring 2022, I had returned from a trip and gave her a call as usual. This time, she said to me, "I've been waiting for you." It was as if the Holy Spirit was saying, "Tilicia, it's time." We prayed, and she thanked the Lord for "the time He has given me and the life He allowed me to live." I will never forget those words. Then she cried, but it was not a cry of sadness. She was ready. There was a great sense of peace in knowing where she had been and where she was going.

There I was, in the awkward and uncomfortable position of saying to Mother Williams (her sister), this is it. I couldn't do it. I was afraid. I feared that it was not my place. I feared that those in the church would say that I was giving up. I wasn't giving up. I knew the Holy Spirit had told me that it was her time. Although I feared what others would say, it felt more important for me to focus on why He would reveal this to me. It was not for me at all. It was for Mother Phillips. I cannot begin to fathom the thoughts or emotions that come with knowing that you are living your literal last days on earth, your last moments. What I do know is that I serve a God who would bring peace to the souls of His children even as He transitions them home. As was the case with Minister Gary, the Holy Spirit sent me to her to ease her transition into her final resting place.

A few days after our call, I awoke from my sleep at 3:38 am. I could not fall back asleep. Later that evening, I received a call. I didn't have to answer; I knew she had passed. I called Mother Phillip's sister. She told me that Mother Phillips called her at three o'clock that morning. She wanted help getting out of bed. Mother Williams helped her and left, and when she returned around 8:00 am, her sister was already gone. Mother Williams was saddened at the idea that her sister had left this earth alone. But I assured her that she was not alone. The Lord had allowed Mother Williams to see her sister just one more time, and I was awakened from my slumber in those precious moments to usher one of the Lord's newest saints into her final resting place. I was not physically present. The Holy Spirit had allowed me to step into His Spirit realm for a farewell to a daughter He was bringing home.

In the days leading up to Mother Phillips' transition, I was at the peak of my spiritual sensitivity and spiritual awareness. I had become so aware of the Holy Spirit's presence that I was at a partial disconnect with this physical world. Imagine closing your eyes and feeling someone's presence standing beside you. That's how close I could feel the Holy Spirit's presence beside me. I recall sitting in my prayer room, praying, spending my quiet time with Him, and then reaching out because a presence *that* palpable had to be physical. And then I remember pulling back, too afraid, yet again, of what would happen if I allowed myself to believe in the unbelievable, the miraculous—the Spirit realm.

When someone is preparing to be with our Heavenly Father, whether a result of illness or old age, they will often speak aloud to someone who is not physically present or able to be seen with the physical eyes of others in the room. My husband once asked me, "What are they seeing?" My response was, "Not what, Who?" The Spirit realm is unveiled, and the Holy Spirit presents Himself to take His children home into our final resting place. My husband's question was no different from our other family members and friends. They want to know "what" the person is seeing when no one else is in the room. How can we believe in God and believe that Heaven exists and not believe that the Holy Spirit can enter our physical realm and be within the mist of our physical space? How can we have disbelief in what cannot be seen with our physical eyes but can be seen with our spiritual eyes? Or is the real issue that many people lack spiritual sight? The foundation of faith is belief. I cannot believe on behalf of my loved ones, nor can I force them to believe. I can only attest to the things the Holy Spirit has allowed me to witness with spiritual eyes, eyes that you cannot use if you do not believe.

In the three days following Mother Phillips' transition, I was in a euphoric state, a dream-like state. In Mother Phillips' transition, the Holy Spirit had shown me peace, a peace that transcends understanding, and it was magnificent. But after the three days had passed, I felt physically drained. I had come down from feeling and sensing everything, including the rich and intense presence of the Holy Spirit. It was as though I had come back to this physical world. I thanked God for using me in this way. For the first time, the Holy Spirit had allowed me to experience Him in a way that had taken a physical toll on my fleshly body.

About a year before Mother Phillips passed, I had reflected on what it truly means to be used by God. I thought about how people say they want to be used by God. But if we truly think about it, I'm not sure we really want Him to use us in the way He desires to use us. Being used by God takes sacrifice and ultimate submission. In my spiritual journey to intimacy with the Holy Spirit, I had been obedient; I had been disciplined. But until that point, I had not reached a place of true sacrifice. After feeling emotionally and physically depleted, I began to wonder if I really wanted to be used by God. I thought, *"Is this what it takes? Is this what it is going to feel like?"* We can accept the invitation to be used, but How He uses us is according to His will and His purpose for our lives. As a human being, a person wrapped in flesh, the task He puts before us, the things He allows us to see, can also be an area where He tests us and grows us.

The women I have described thus far, Minister Gary and Mother Phillips, are part of a list of women whom the Lord has placed into my life throughout the years. Minnie Harrington, Mari Evans, Thelma Davis, Evelyn Chavers. These are all older women who have been in my life at various stages of my life. It would be a careless oversight on my part if I did not recognize and acknowledge the connection I have with older women. The Lord brings me into their lives for a reason that is typically unbeknownst to me but is often revealed, either to them or to me later.

Ms. Minnie-- When I first met Ms. Minnie, it was at my first full-time job at a local health department. It was my first position out of college. I was seated in the cubicle next to hers. When I sat down the first day, Ms. Minnie turned and looked at me. She said, "The Lord sent you here to work with me so that I wouldn't have to retire." Quite naturally, I was surprised, shocked even, but I went along with it and just said, "OK." Ms. Minnie needed to work five more years before becoming eligible for medical coverage through Medicare. However, in a world where technology changes nearly every second of the day, Ms. Minnie struggled to keep up. That's where I came in. I was adept with computers, but I was even better at offering instruction. It seems to be an area where my patience falls into place. I worked with Ms. Minnie for five years, and she retired. Three years after her retirement, Ms. Minnie passed.

Mari Evans—Mari Evans is a woman who, like Mother Phillips, I never had the pleasure to meet in person but would come to know her as a friend. Mari Evans was a world-renowned poet, and she had my heart. In my role at the health department, I would have to call Ms. Evans at her home. We would talk, but she never mentioned her success in poetry until I left the health department. She lived in a rough neighborhood. Ms. Evans was literally a pearl residing in an oyster of a neighborhood. I was supposed to call her with work-related discussions, but the Lord had a different goal. I continued to talk with her after my departure from the health department and until her death just a few years later. I never expected to form a bond with someone I never met in person. The Lord had done it once again. He brought her into life during the final days of her life.

Thelma Davis—My great-grandmother, Thelma Davis, was a woman with whom I did not develop a relationship until I was an adult, after the passing of my grandmother. She had spoken with my grandmother every day for decades. When my grandmother passed, I wanted my great-grandmother to have a piece of her daughter. So, I stepped in. My great-grandmother had difficulty hearing. When no one else had the patience to hold a conversation with her, I did. In fact, I took pride in speaking loudly so she could easily hear me. In public, people would stare, but I did not mind. I did for her what I hoped someone would be willing to do for me if I lived to be 80 years old with difficulty hearing. I was patient, and I spoke loudly. This had to be the inner workings of the Holy Spirit because I do not have a loud voice. I have more of a calming voice, but for her, I was willing to adapt so that she would have someone to speak with. I had phone calls with my great-grandmother consistently for four years. She looked forward to my calls. That made me feel good.

After she passed, I realized that the calls I began making for her became calls I looked forward to. After those four years, she was gone.

Mother Evelyn — Mother Evelyn is a woman who is very much alive. I met her in 2018, and I did not say much to her or anyone else in the church. In early 2019, she approached me in church and told me that the Lord sent me, not just to her, but for her, if indeed I was the type of person she thought I was. She did not describe the type of person she thought I was, but I went with it. It reminded me of the first interaction I had with Ms. Minnie. As time went on, she and I developed a spiritual kinship, and oftentimes, those around us refer to me as one of her armor-bearers. One night, on our prayer call, she described a pain in her lower back and hip from a sciatic nerve. One of the gifts that the Holy Spirit operates through Mother Evelyn is the gift of healing. But she told us that after praying for the healing of so many others, this pain was meant to be healed by someone else. She said that God wanted someone to bring healing to her. At that moment, I thought, *"What if that person was me? What if the Lord wanted me to pray for her? That's silly, right? The Holy Spirit has not given me this gift."*

A few months later, something stirred within me. I felt compelled to call Mother Evelyn and pray. It would be the first time that I had ever prayed with someone for their healing. Afterward, I was anxious. She was headed to the doctor the following day, and I was afraid that she would call to tell me that she couldn't get the treatment she needed. She had been waiting all these months, and yet I, of all people, was the person who prayed for her healing. Later that day, she called me. She was finally able to get the shot she needed for the pain. We were elated! The Lord had answered this prayer. But was it a coincidence? I don't believe in coincidences, yet there I was, doubting what the Holy Spirit had done. I had prayed to Him for a miracle, observed the miracle, and then doubted what was right in front of me. It reminded me of the Israelites. The Lord asked Moses, "Will they never believe me, even after all the miraculous signs I have done among them?" (Numbers 14:11, NLT). Despite God's promises and the wonders they had witnessed, they refused to believe what was right in front of them.

What if I had not overcome my fear and decided not to pray? Why did I wait so long to pray with her? I felt the guilt of waiting. I didn't think I could be someone the Holy Spirit would use to pray for healing in others. But I was grateful. I was grateful that the Lord brought healing and relief to Mother Evelyn. Even more, I was grateful that He allowed me to be a witness and to take part in His great works. About a month later, I was in church, and the pastor asked me to come up and touch Mother Evelyn's hips while he prayed for her. For me, this was confirmation, not confirmation on a specific spiritual gift, but confirmation that the Holy Spirit was using me, and that was more than enough for me. At that moment, I realized that I needed to stop waiting for it to feel right and to stop questioning why or how the Holy Spirit was using me to get His work done.

A City on a Hill

> *You are the light of the world. A city*
> *set on a hill cannot be hidden.* (Matthew

There were times when I sought the Holy Spirit for affirmation of my spiritual gifts. During one of these moments, I attended church. It was what seemed to be a typical day at church, i.e., no special occasions or holidays. Many of us were standing in line to sow a seed. For the first time, the pastor called on me to comfort others in the line. I stepped out, and the pastor asked me to wrap my arms around a young lady, Erica, so she would know she was loved. She began to cry. Later, I would learn that Erica felt loved, and she needed comfort. I did not know it at the time, but the Lord had assigned me to Erica long before this moment.

As I stood back in line, the pastor began to pray for another woman, Courtney. I did not know Courtney, but I could not help but feel her emotions. I began to sob uncontrollably. I had a range of emotions that were not my own. This should have been an opportunity for me to go to her. The Holy Spirit was trying to use me at that moment to reach out to one of His sheep, but I didn't; I couldn't. I was paralyzed. I was paralyzed by the confusion of emotions that stirred within me, by the fear of rejection from this woman who did not know me. I had empathized with others in their pain. But this was different. I was experiencing the impossible, and I could not handle it. The fear of the work that the Holy Spirit was trying to do within me got the best of me.

When it was my turn to approach the pastor, he held my hand and said that the Lord wanted me to be seen, that I am a city on a hill that cannot be hidden. He said I have so much light to share with others because the Lord uses me to shine His light. *"...A city set on a hill cannot be hidden."* (Matthew 5:14, ESV). *I cannot be hidden.* My husband, Johnny, always tells me that people see me. Not only am I someone who had not felt seen, but I also did not have an interest in being seen. My request to the Holy Spirit had been that He would shine His light through me, and others would not see me but see HIM. On that day, the Holy Spirit filled me, and my Heavenly Father honored my request. Now, I need to walk in the confidence to share His light and edify His people. This meant not necessarily overcoming the fear but having the faith to move forward through the fear the same way that the Lord doesn't extinguish the fire, but He walks through it with us. The fire isn't gone. We simply need to have the faith to walk through it and to trust that the Holy Spirit will walk through it with us.

For a moment, I want to take you back to the story of Erica. When I first placed my arms around Erica, it was to bring her comfort as my pastor had instructed me to do. At the time, the Lord did not send me a word for Erica. It wasn't until weeks later that the Holy Spirit allowed me to see her. When the Lord sends me a word for someone, I develop a sense of tunnel vision around that person. My heart beats fast; I am overwhelmed with emotions, and I begin to see that person as if they are the only person in the room, even if we are not in the same room. I had been traveling out of town visiting family, and I realized that once I returned, I needed to approach Erica and tell her that the Lord wanted her to know that He sees her. That moment came during Bible study.

Erica would sit in the back of the church during Bible study. Mostly, she remained quiet. I was nervous to approach her, but I was obedient. I repositioned from my seat toward the front of the church and found a seat in the row behind Erica. I wrote out a note asking her if I could speak with her after the Bible study. She smiled and nodded affirmatively. "Why?" I wondered. "Why would the Lord want me to speak with this young lady?" The answer came sooner than I thought. At the end of Bible study, our pastor asks us what we learned. Almost unknowingly, Erica responded with her story. The words just rolled off her tongue. As it turned out, it was the answer I needed. Erica had just completed her master's degree at the university where I taught. She had been admitted to a doctoral program but was unable to acquire funding for the tuition. In addition, she had recently received a health diagnosis. As a professor, I have helped countless students through these types of challenges. This information made it clear why the Lord placed this young woman on my mind and in my heart. She was someone I could help. She was someone I could mentor. I am grateful that I had already decided to be obedient even before I knew the details of Erica's struggles. Today, Erica is a doctoral student in a Doctor of Psychology program. She was obedient to the Holy Spirit, and once again, He allowed me to bear witness to His great works.

One of the greatest lessons I have learned since I began to recognize the Holy Spirit's voice is that it's not about me. Up to that point, I had been concerned about my internal fears, the fear of judgment, the fear of unbelief, and the fear of rejection. The truth is that allowing these fears to get the best of me prevented me from serving God and fulfilling His purpose for my life. After all, the Lord says, *"For I am the Lord your God who takes hold of your right hand... Do not fear; I will help you."* (Isaiah 41:13, NIV). When the Holy Spirit gives His instruction, particularly around encouraging or reaching out to someone with a word or good deed, it could be life-changing for that person. It could mean the difference between life and death. Who am I to allow my insecurities or discomfort to get in the way of that? Our disobedience costs others their blessing.

Chapter 3:
You Didn't Know How He Would Use You

But as it is written: "Eye has not seen, nor ear heard,
Nor have entered into the heart of man, The things which God
has prepared for those who love Him."
1 Corinthians 2:9 (NIV)

I previously mentioned the Bishop explained that there are levels to this thing, yet he didn't explain what "this" was. I did not understand. What are my spiritual gifts, and what is God trying to show me by allowing me to experience His gifts? From my literal knowledge, I understood that one of my motivational gifts was exhortation. I understood that the Holy Spirit had operated through me by allowing me to be an exhorter. He supernaturally enables me to inspire others to allow the light that shines within them to be released so that they may be edified. However, this did not capture all that the Holy Spirit has allowed me to experience. Mother Evelyn had additional insight for me. She said, "You are not only an exhorter, but you have other gifts as well. You are a seer." I was stunned, speechless. This was the perfect opportunity to "lean not on thine own understanding." Yet, that's what I did. I had to learn more about the role of the seer. I knew the literal meaning of this term, but what did SHE mean when using this term to describe a spiritual gift?

The Holy Spirit allows us to see things differently through our spiritual eyes. In the Old Testament, a seer is a specific type of prophet. They saw the hidden truths the Lord revealed to them. I receive this, Lord. I receive this gift from you. For as long as I can remember, I have seen things differently. I have prayed, "Holy Spirit, remove the veil from my eyes, remove the veil from my ears, that I might see with my spiritual eyes and hear with my spiritual ears." Through the church, I've interacted with many women. When they speak or pray, the Holy Spirit manifests through me, and suddenly, their spiritual gifts are revealed to me. I can perceive in them the things they may not see in themselves. I perceive how the Holy Spirit manifests within them to use them, and I can hear what the Holy Spirit says about them. Not what He says to them, but what He says about them. It's through this impartation from the Holy Spirit that I am able to encourage others. He shows me, and then He says, "Now tell them."

First Corinthians says, *"But he who prophesies speaks edification and exhortation and comfort to men."* (14:3, NIV).

Could this revelation from a woman the Holy Spirit has manifested through her entire life be the key to everything I had felt in recent years? That the Lord had called me to be a seer? It occurred to me that the Prophet Samuel, a seer in the Old Testament, first experienced God speaking directly to him in a land called Shiloh. When Mother Evelyn offered this revelation to me, I lived on a street named Shiloh. In the Bible, Samuel takes a rock, a stone, and names it Ebenezer, saying, "This far the Lord has helped us." When I first began to journal, to chronicle my life, the Lord led me to name my journals. I named them "Ebenezer" because I wanted them to serve as a reminder of all the Lord had brought me through and all that the Lord was bringing me to. These may all seem like coincidences. But I was convinced that this had to be God's handiwork. I asked, "Lord, what do you want me to do with this? How does this fit within your purpose for my life? How do I use this to bring your people to you and your kingdom to me?"

On our prayer line, we do praise reports. During one of these calls, I had a lot to be grateful for. My praise report was on my growing spiritual connection with the Holy Spirit. A celebration that the Lord would awaken me out of my sleep to speak with Him. Ms. Cherry, a woman from church, told me that this was why He kept calling me. She was right. The Lord wanted me to know that He missed our time together. But the important part is that the Lord wanted to reach out to me, and He knew how to reach out to me. I began to feel the Holy Spirit take hold of me. Ms. Cherry calls it "an awakening." I had gone from not knowing or understanding what spiritual gifts were, to recognizing that I can experience and do supernatural works as the Holy Spirit operates in His power through me. This revelation was an awakening moment that led me to reflect on my relationship with Mother Evelyn.

Mother Evelyn and I have a spiritual relationship. We have a shared bond in our sensitivity to the Holy Spirit. Further, she believes the Lord intended for us to have a spiritual connection with one another. One night, she called me to inform me that the Lord had told her that I would be the Aaron to her, Moses. First, let's take a moment to process. "Who says this to someone?!" I felt both the pressure and honor that she would view me in this way. But what did this mean? What did this mean for our relationship? God speaks to her, and she needed me to speak to others on her behalf. God spoke to Moses, and Moses spoke to Aaron. In doing so, Aaron was there to witness God speak to and through Moses. I liken myself to Aaron in that he was quickly obedient to God's instruction. Aaron was also a good listener. I recall Mother Evelyn asking me if I was a good listener. Aaron's upbringing and experiences made him a better listener of the people despite his pitfalls. I suppose that if Moses were a better speaker, he would have gone directly to the people. But God knew that Aaron had better insight into the people and that they would respond to him.

Why would God continue to offer instruction to Moses without healing his speech? The Lord says, "Who gives speech to man?" So, perhaps the speech issue is not really a crutch. An act of disobedience, yes. But consider that it could have been God's way of doing things according to His will. Aaron not only helps Moses. Aaron begins to hear a word from God, but only after experiencing God through traveling with Moses and speaking the messages the Lord revealed to Moses. While Aaron may not be the person called by God, being in the presence and proximity of the chosen one allowed a residual effect on Aaron and a more intimate relationship with the Lord.

In the Bible, Moses is a central figure. He is the person God chooses to speak directly to. He even gets to see the Lord. Aaron and Joshua served Moses. They went where he went. Moses gives messages to Aaron from the Lord as if Aaron is receiving the word directly from Him. In the church, I serve Mother Evelyn. For this reason, I have conversations with her that others may not get an opportunity to have. I get to witness when God uses her to bring a *word of prophecy*. All of this is possible through my service. There were times when Aaron misstepped, but the Lord also chose Aaron. He made him a priest; He began to speak to him directly. My point is that it's our service that invites the Lord to speak to us, to encounter His Holy presence. Through my service, the Holy Spirit has allowed me to bear witness to miraculous works that *eyes have not seen and ears have not heard* (1 Corinthians 2:9).

Mother Evelyn wholeheartedly believes that God sent me to her. There was a point when I believed her simply because she told me. I trusted that she was someone God spoke to directly. But as time went on, I began to believe, not because of what she said, but because the Holy Spirit told me Himself. When we consider God's will and God's purpose for our lives, so many of us limit our purpose to the time we have here in this earthly realm. To think that God's purpose for our lives is limited to our time on earth is to think small, too small, in my opinion. We know that God is not bound by time; He is not bound by the physical spaces in which we live. So why would we believe that He created us for a purpose that is bound by time and space? Just as the Lord prepares us for a purpose here on earth, our time on earth should prepare us for our purpose in His heavenly kingdom. Many will be blessed to enter the kingdom of heaven, but not everyone who enters will have a role. Mother Evelyn has a desire not only to teach but to be the best teacher. This desire, this motivation, is not just for this earthly realm. For several decades and to many generations, she has been just that, a great teacher. But, one day, it will be her turn to return to glory and teach God's people, to teach within the kingdom. I serve her so that one day, she will be prepared to fulfill this role to live out her ultimate purpose. I pray that one day, I receive a double portion of this teaching spirit.

You might be thinking, "It is such a blessing for the Lord to use you in this way, to be in a position to help this woman for her ultimate assignment from the Lord." I received this, but honestly, when the Lord told me why He sent me to Mother Evelyn, I was heartbroken. It meant that the Lord had called me for this assignment until He calls her home. It means that once again, I will experience a spiritual relationship with someone to support them spiritually, and in the end, I will be left here to mourn them. The irony in this situation is that she knows this. Just as the Lord had revealed my calling to help her on this God-given mission, the Lord had also revealed to Mother Evelyn that I was the person He sent to help her prepare for it. In her words, "Helping me won't make my death date come any sooner than the Lord wants it to. When it happens, it will be the right time." So like Aaron did for Moses, I serve her, *as unto the Lord*.

The Good News

In my professional role as a professor and researcher, I started out impatient. I wanted to be successful in my research. Like many millennials, I wanted it to happen right away. God had very different plans for me. In the first few years, I spent a great deal of my time helping students achieve the type of success I wanted to achieve. It took everything in me, and everything that I felt wasn't in me, to set aside my desires and patiently wait for what I wanted so that I could focus on mentoring my students and offering guidance to them. The students were my focus because that was where God placed me. If I could go back even just four years, I would tell myself that the Lord will open the windows of heaven and pour out blessings in such quantities that you will not have room enough to receive them. The Lord brings us to our blessings, to our promises, to our purposes through His process. What are we willing to go through so that we may share a testimony and the good news with God's sheep? What are we willing to sacrifice so that the Lord can use it? Many of the trials we endure are not for us. Our sufferings are not for us but for God to use us to be a blessing to others.

Many people pray that God will use them, but if we reflect on what that could mean, we may find that we really, genuinely do not want to be used by God. If the Lord gives a glimpse of the future, a vision, or a promise, we are excited, and we are all in. But what if God were to show us the process part—the sufferings and sacrifices we must endure to have that expected end? Illness, heartbreak, loss, abuse, and then there's that issue of time and delays. Lord, I am willing to endure the trials and tribulations, but for how long? How long? Yes, I want to be used as a vessel by the Lord so that I may be a benefit to others during their times of suffering. So, as I reflect, I want to tell my younger self, "Just wait, He's coming. And He will use you to raise up, to edify His people. Finish the race and complete the task the Lord God has given you, the task of testifying to the Good News of God's grace. Amen."

Chapter 4:
The Enemy Creeps In

[8] Be sober-minded; be watchful. Your adversary the devil prowls around like a roaring lion, seeking someone to devour. [9] Resist him, firm in your faith, knowing that the same kinds of suffering are being experienced by your brotherhood throughout the world (1 Peter 5:8-9, ESV).

There are times when the Lord goes silent on me. During prayer, He does not speak. I stop feeling the Holy Spirit's presence in the way that I usually feel Him. During this time, the enemy creeps in. God had been affirming all my encounters, letting me know that they were real. However, once those around me affirmed and encouraged me not to be afraid of the judgment of others, I transitioned to a state of inner conflict. I began to tell myself that I should not desire the gifts of the Holy Spirit. That it would not be humble of me to desire the Holy Spirit to operate through me. I told myself that I really had not heard from God. The enemy knows our insecurities. He knows where we are most vulnerable. He knows the things that cause us to have self-doubt. I value humility. So, if anything ever made me feel arrogant, I would remove it. And so, he crept in. I began to doubt myself, doubting that the Lord would want to use me in this way. I began to wonder if my emotions resulted from not understanding certain spiritual gifts and my apprehension towards embracing the gifts.

I was cautioned that what I thought I had sensed as humility could be false humility. This was one of the ways that the enemy tried to keep me from the place that God was calling me to. If I would give in to the thoughts of unworthiness, the idea that God only works through pastors, bishops, and priests in this way, then the enemy could get me to a stagnant place. He could keep me in a place where not only my spiritual growth would be stunted, but I could potentially revert to a place of hiding—hiding from my calling, hiding from my belief in the spirit realm, and maybe even denying that the Lord really does speak to me. It occurred to me that this wasn't humility at all. This was pride. That's a familiar area of comfort. Pride. I was not jumping at the first opportunity to share "my gifts" with the world or seeking to make a grand announcement about miraculous signs and wonders. However, the thoughts and emotions that kept me from fully embracing my calling from the Holy Spirit; logic, fear of rejection, fear of judgment, and criticism, were various ways that pride was manifesting. When we fail to see pride, when we fail to acknowledge the presence of pride in our actions, it becomes a powerful tool for the enemy to use against us.

During this time of inner conflict, I recall sitting in church. There was a woman there preparing to sow seed (a financial offering to the church). The pastor prayed for her. Immediately, I was overcome with emotion. I didn't feel sympathy for her or even empathize with her. In fact, I did not feel my own emotions at all. I felt her emotions. It did not feel good. Through this experience, I learned that on paper, having spiritual gifts revealed is beautiful and to desire spiritual gifts even more so. But that does not mean it feels good. I acknowledge that for some, it's an incredible feeling. But for the rest of us, it can be scary. It feels uncontrollable. Of course. It makes sense that it would feel uncontrollable as we are not operating in our own power. I had heard it so many times, "Lean not to thine own understanding." Once again, I thought, *"Holy Spirit, what do you want me to do with this, this gift of feeling someone else's emotions?"*

I thought that feeling the emotions of others was somehow tied to the spiritual gift of exhortation or even discerning of spirits, but I did not have a definitive answer. The Holy Spirit allows me to see people, on the inside, not for who they are, but I see what God has placed in them. I see their spirit. It's as if my spiritual eyes won't allow my physical eyes to see the flesh in front of me. At times, I thought this was God showing me His heart. He shows me how He sees the person. For this reason, it seemed less important to label the specific spiritual gift and more important to accept that this was one way the Spirit trusted He could use me.

Spiritual Things Don't Make Sense

One Sunday morning, I attended a church service. The pastor mentioned that spiritual things don't make sense. This resonated with me. Oftentimes, my pastor will speak about not relying on your intellect. This particular comment was an example of the importance of not trying to rationalize or explain the inner workings of the Holy Spirit. I found his comment useful at that moment in my journey. I was reminded of Fuchsia Pickett's perspective on *Doubting Thomas*. A common perspective on this story is to focus on the idea that Thomas did not believe that Jesus revealed Himself to the disciples. I agree with this. However, Fuchsia offered another perspective: no one can experience intimacy with the Holy Spirit on your behalf. Other people cannot experience the Holy Spirit for you. That's how I felt about my spiritual journey. Not only was I experiencing things that I could not comprehend, but I also could not formulate the words to describe my experience to others. Likewise, if someone would have tried to explain to me experiencing an encounter with the Holy Spirit, there are no words they could utter that would help me grasp or imagine that experience.

I had three women to help me through my encounters and my fears (Mother Evelyn, Ms. Cherry, and Dr. Enola). I call these women my *"Peter, James,* and *John."* My pastor recommends that one of the keys to getting through tough times and ensuring spiritual growth is to surround yourself with people who are willing to go through those tough times with you, support you, and pray with you. For Jesus, this was Peter, James, and John. Although there were twelve disciples, the Gospels teach us that there were some places where Jesus only took Peter, James, and John (Mark 5:37). Jesus did not take the twelve everywhere He went. No, I am not Jesus, and they are not disciples, but these women were older, they were wise, and they had accepted their invitation to receive their unique gifts from the Holy Spirit.

When we go through tough times, we need people to hold us up. It may not be appropriate to invite our full circle of friends or family. When I went through a season of spiritual vulnerability, when I began to experience the Holy Spirit's gifts, to say that I was fearful is an understatement. To overcome my fear, accept my calling, and obey God's will for my life, I needed a "*Peter, James,* and *John."* Who is in your inner circle? Who are the people who pour into your life spiritually? Who are the people you can be vulnerable with when it comes to matters of the heart but also matters of the spirit?

The most important characteristic of these women is that they, too, were afraid when they were initially offered the gifts of the Holy Spirit. These women reminded me that when the Lord chooses someone to receive these gifts (as He had chosen me), rather than being afraid, I should embrace the invitation and make the choice to accept the anointing on my life and the blessings that would benefit others as a result of the choice I make. The women were my trusted confidantes. During the precarious time in my life of the revelation of spiritual gifts, I could be vulnerable with these women. As was the case with Jesus, when I shared with these women my encounters with the Holy Spirit, experiences I felt that no one would believe, I trusted that I had their discretion, and they would keep my words near their hearts (Mark 5:43; Mark 9:9). The thought of this brought me a great depth of inner peace. If you could imagine putting on the full armor of the Lord, these women served as the breastplate of righteousness to protect my heart, the shield of faith to block the naysayers, and the shoes of peace to keep me moving forward (Ephesians 6:10-18).

When I met these women, each of them reached out to me in their own way. Mother Evelyn is the lead Mother of the church I attend. She is a woman in her 70s who grew up in the South. She has been committed to the church her entire life. Many people will attest to her spiritual gift of prophecy, while others know her for her gift of teachings. Some people even refer to her as a prophetess. Ms. Cherry is a church member and Evangelist. I first met Ms. Cherry at a women's meeting. She was a complete sweetheart. Ms. Cherry has three daughters, who prepared her for a ministry that would reach out to young women. She has a gift for interpreting dreams. Ms. Cherry is open to allowing the Holy Spirit to use her in any way He sees fit, including bringing a prophetic word. Lastly, Dr. Enola is an English teacher by profession and a teacher in ministry. Dr. Enola and I share similarities in our initial response to the Holy Spirit's calling. She has the gift of speaking in tongues and the Spirit uses her to interpret tongues. Dr. Enola is also a writer and poet. Observing this talent in her allowed me to understand how the Holy Spirit will use the giftings of writing and speech to work in concert to bring His word.

While it was a blessing to have the support and guidance of these women, it was not sufficient. They could be WITH me on my walk, but they could not experience the walk FOR me. Part of the walk that leads us to intimacy with the Holy Spirit is belief—belief in a spiritual world that many do not believe exists. But it's also a belief that God allows us to cross over into that spiritual realm. It sounded silly, and I expected people to call me insane. Ms. Cherry told me, "It's not that you didn't know the Lord would use you. It's that you didn't know HOW the Lord would use you." She was right. Her words were profound and pierced right through my heart. I did not expect THIS. Honestly, I don't know what I expected, and at the time, I did not ask the Holy Spirit why He allowed me to draw nearer to Him in His realm. I was confounded by what the Holy Spirit was doing with me and what He wanted me to do. I simply asked, "Holy Spirit, what do you want me to do with this?"

I would love to say that being in a space of spiritual sensitivity only brought me feelings of joy. However, the closer I felt to the Spirit realm, the more disconnected I felt from those

No one can experience the Holy Spirit on our behalf.

around me. Like the disciple Thomas, this was personal. This was something between me and the Holy Spirit. Thomas doubted the other disciples who had an encounter with Jesus. For generations, Thomas has been touted as the disciple who did not believe, even earning the nickname "Doubting Thomas." But perhaps there is another lesson to be gleaned here. Just as Thomas needed to see Jesus for himself, other people cannot experience the Holy Spirit on our behalf. No one could experience Him on my behalf. I had to stop trying to make sense of how the Spirit was working in my life. I had to learn to trust Him when things don't make sense and to accept that through Him, all things are possible. As often as I have heard and recited the scripture, "Through Christ, all things are possible," I had taken for granted what the word "ALL" really means. 'All things are possible' does not mean the things we believe are possible. 'All things are possible' includes the things we never conceived were possible.

Focus on Him

Let your eyes look straight ahead; fix your gaze directly before you. Give careful thought to the paths for your feet and be steadfast in all your ways. [27] Do not turn to the right or the left; keep your foot from evil. Proverbs 4:25-27 NIV

I would be remiss if I only spoke about encounters with the Holy Spirit but did not speak about the presence of another spirit. The enemy lurks even when the Lord is seeking intimacy with His children. The Bible tells us that we are in spiritual warfare (Ephesians 6:12). We know that the enemy is present. He creeps into our minds and our thoughts. While I know this to be true, I had never FELT the enemy's presence. At the time, the Holy Spirit allowed me to discern this spirit, but I did not know this was possible. The Holy Spirit began to allow me to become spiritually sensitive. Around the time of Mother Phillips' passing, I knew the Holy Spirit was present, but I sensed another spirit in the room, one that I did not invite and surely was not invited.

I sought out Mother Evelyn to discuss this issue of the other presence in the room. I did not know it at the time, but I was experiencing a discerning of spirits. I had heard of this spiritual gift, but no one had ever described it to me, how it would feel, or how you know when it happens. Without that explanation, I felt something was wrong. My senses were overwhelmed. I felt a heaviness of emotions. It was the feeling of being alone in a room with your back turned or your eyes closed, and then someone comes into the room. There is no one physically there, and yet, you feel that someone is there. It was unlike the palpable presence of the Holy Spirit. It lurked with a desire to go unnoticed.

Mother Evelyn told me that this was a good thing. "How can this be a good thing?" I asked. She said it's only bad when the enemy is present and seeking to devour you without your awareness or knowledge. By acknowledging the presence of evil spirits, I can speak to them, confront them, and cast them out. She encouraged me through this experience and told me that I need not be afraid. From there, I knew I needed to seek out the Holy Spirit. I knew I needed His counsel. Once again, I went to the Holy Spirit in my quiet time, a time that is not reserved for me to speak but to listen. So, I uttered the words of the Prophet Samuel, "Speak, Lord, for your servant listens."

The Holy Spirit was quite clear in His instruction. *Tilicia, focus on me. Do not look to the left or right; instead, look straight ahead.* He was telling me not to be distracted. The enemy is present to distract us from our instruction, our service, and our purpose. My initial thoughts were indeed centered on the enemy, "Where did you come from here? Why are you here?" But the Holy Spirit did not allow me to focus on that. He was saying, "Don't worry about Satan; he really doesn't matter. I need you to focus on me and the task I've set before you." What has the Holy Spirit asked you to do, but distractions have kept you from being obedient? If I had not remained focused, I could not have been there for Mother Williams and I could not have been there for Mother Phillips in her last days. Sometimes, the tasks that the Lord puts before us are not for our benefit but for the benefit of His other sheep, His children. It's not our job to know who needs what, when, why, or how. That is the work of the Holy Spirit. Our role is to be sensitive to the Spirit and be obedient when the instruction comes.

Fuchsia Pickett

I've mentioned Fuchsia Pickett quite a bit thus far. This name will be an ongoing part of my life. When I first met with the Bishop, he recommended that I read books by Fuchsia Picket. He said that there are levels to spiritual gifts. I had decided to read a particular book, but when a different book arrived first, *Receiving Divine Revelation*, I took it as a sign that this was what the Lord wanted me to read. Fuchsia describes the experiences of her new birth. It was as if she lifted the words out of my journal, out of my thoughts, and placed them in her book. God could not have had a better way to affirm all that He was speaking to me and connecting with me than to have me read the accounts of another person. I thought, *"Ok, Lord, spiritual gifts, yes, I get it, now what?"* I've come to understand that through the Holy Spirit, the possibilities are limitless. Honestly, the "what" is not as important as knowing that I get to experience God while I am still here on earth. What a blessing!

The Test

> *Blessed is the one who perseveres under trial because, having stood the test, that person will receive the crown of life that the Lord has promised to those who love him.* James 1:12

Until now, I have discussed various encounters with the Holy Spirit and how He operates through me. I must touch on the season of my life when the Lord began an awakening in me and the circumstances. Many of us will be tested before we hear the Lord's voice. For me, this was a test of obedience during a time of trials in my life. Toward the end of 2021, my husband was informed that he might have prostate cancer. During this time, we had casually discussed trying to get pregnant. We knew that if the cancer had returned, surgery would be the only option. This would mean that we could not conceive a child naturally. Immediately, I flew into gear. We scheduled a fertility appointment in hopes of conceiving using an alternative method. During the first appointment, I found out that I had a uterine fibroid and a low egg reserve. Despite being in my mid-30s, I had the egg count of a woman in her mid-40s. I was devastated.

As it turned out, my husband had advanced prostate cancer, and the possibility of having a child seemed to dwindle away. At that moment, I felt hopeless. I felt that I had served God, I had been diligent, and this was how He repaid me. There was no way for me to view the situation other than, "God hates me." I really thought that. "God hates me." First, Peter says, "For you know that God paid a ransom to save you from the empty life you inherited" (1 Peter 1:18, NIV). How could God hate me yet love me enough to prepay a blood ransom to save me? But He didn't both hate me and love me. He just loved me. But to be honest, knowing He loved me did not help how I felt. There was a lesson to be learned here. I didn't know what that lesson was yet.

In writing this book, you may be expecting me to say that God answered my prayers, that my husband was cured of cancer, and that we were able to conceive a child. That is not the case. But God did come through. I responded to my circumstances the way many of us do. I cried. I asked God, "Why?" I felt like I had done His work; I had been of service. I had sacrificed so much of my time for His people, to encourage them, to teach them. I had enjoyed serving His people. Yet, there I was, once again, taking another blow of life. At that time, I decided to take a step back from my service to the church. I called into the prayer line and announced that I would not be facilitating the calls and focus on me, on giving myself time, or so I thought.

When I announced that I was stepping down from the prayer line, it felt wrong. I felt the guilt eating away at my spirit. I prayed to the Lord, asking for His forgiveness. I felt responsible for the spiritual growth of the women on the prayer line. What would happen if their spiritual growth was stunted because of my decision? It did not take long (a few days) before the Lord called out to me. He told me that I could take a break from facilitating the calls, but I could not leave the calls. I could not leave the women's ministry. It may seem that this was just guilt eating away at me, but when the Holy Spirit speaks, you know it's Him. Therefore, I needed to make another decision: Should I obey or disobey the instruction of the Holy Spirit? Little did I know, the Lord had brought me into a crisis, a test, but if I passed, it would lead to an ultimate invitation into an intimacy with the Holy Spirit that I didn't even know was possible. Fuchsia Pickett says,

We don't know who we are until God takes us through the testing and we see our response. The wilderness we are in is God's classroom. When it looks black and hopeless, we may be tempted to think God doesn't love us. On the contrary, He loves us so much He is training us to bring us to spiritual maturity so that we can receive our inheritance. *Fuchsia Pickett, p. 114, God's Purpose for You.*[4]

The week after stepping down from facilitating the prayer call, I called back in. The women were excited to hear my voice. They were my great cloud of witnesses. People could observe and attest to the work that the Holy Spirit was doing in my life, even when it hurt. How could anyone bear witness to great news, the good news of God's blessings in my life, if I didn't let them in? In order to share the good news of God's grace, I needed to do exactly that—share. I have never been one to share good news or bad news. One of my favorite scriptures says, *"But to do good and communicate forget not, for with such sacrifices God is well pleased."* (Hebrews 13:16, KJV). The women on the prayer line were there for me, even when they did not know all the details. I trusted them enough to think of them as the Apostle Paul thought of the Philippians, *"We are in this struggle together. You have seen my struggle in the past, and you know that I am still in the midst of it."* (Philippians 1:30, NLT). I was in the midst of it. I was in a place where I needed God's people, His witnesses, to come with me as I sojourned through the midst of trials and tribulations until I reached the Lord's expected end for me.

---

[4] *Fuchsia Pickett, p. 114, God's Purpose for You.*

I learned the value of sharing my struggles with others. It allowed me to personally understand how communication could be a sacrifice. Sharing with others who are willing to lift me up in my time of need prevented me from giving up and quitting. Giving up or giving in is exactly what the enemy wants us to do. My greatest purpose in this life is to exhort others, to call out the potential and possibilities in them that they may not see in themselves. By showing up for the prayer call, I did not feel as though I was putting the needs of others ahead of my own. I felt that I was being of service to my Heavenly Father, even in the midst of my fire. In doing so, I was obedient; I was focused on helping others instead of focusing on my pain. I was going about my Father's business. *"...to obey is better than sacrifice."* (1 Samuel 15:22, NIV). By doing this, I had passed the test before me, which would lead to the Holy Spirit's invitation to get to know my Heavenly Father more intimately.

Experiencing the Holy Spirit

> *The wind blows wherever it pleases. You hear its sound, but you cannot tell where it comes from or where it is going. So it is with everyone born of the Spirit.* (John 3:8, NIV)

How does it feel to experience the Holy Ghost, the Holy Spirit? I recall trying to explain to the Bishop how I felt in my "spiritual encounters." The best explanation I could provide was that I feel like I am not in control, that I no longer have control over my body. It was not what I had expected. I did not shout. I did not scream. I still don't. This may be part of the reason it took me so long to reach out to someone. When your experiences and reactions are not similar to those around you and are not how others describe them, you begin to question if your experiences are valid. I thought, *"I could not have really felt the Holy Spirit's presence. Right?"* This is the reason God led me to write this book. My experiences did not compare to those described by others. Yet, I knew I could not be the only person to feel this way.

To make matters worse, the idea of letting go and allowing the Holy Spirit to take over terrified me. There had been times when I felt the Holy Spirit's presence, and I began to move in response. In those moments, I think, "No, this doesn't feel right." But how should it feel?

Is there anyone who is the authority on your personal experience of the Holy Spirit? When the disciples saw Jesus (John 20:19-29), Thomas was not present. When he had heard of Jesus' presence, Thomas wanted to experience Jesus for himself. I cannot verify if anyone around me has truly experienced the Holy Spirit. I can only describe my experience. When the Holy Spirit manifests His power through me, I am in complete submission. My thoughts are not my thoughts; my actions are not my actions. I am completely filled with an inexplicable emotion. There is a joy inside of me that compels me to tears. My heart races. My senses awaken in ways I did not know were possible. I feel the Holy Spirit as if He is physically standing right beside me. I am reminded of the conversation between Jesus and Nicodemus. Jesus states, "I have spoken to you of earthly things, and you do not believe; how then will you believe if I speak of heavenly things?" (John 3:12, NIV). But just before this, Jesus likens the Spirit's birth to the wind. The wind comes, and it goes. You do not know where it came from, you do not know where it is going, but you are aware that it was here, that it happened. The experience of the Holy Spirit operating through you can be inexplicable and indescribable, but when He does, there is no doubt that you have been filled.

I have the greatest discernment of the Holy Spirit's presence when He operates through others in my presence. If someone prays and the Holy Spirit moves through them with a gift of prayer, I discern His presence, even if the person has not recognized their gift or recognized that the Holy Spirit operates within them. The same occurs when someone speaks in tongues or provides a prophecy in my presence. I feel the Holy Spirit breathe through like a gust of wind, illuminating the person He is operating through. In that moment, I know that He is there, and through people, I see Him. Through others, I see His heart.

I have come to embrace the perceiving of God's presence. However, I did not quite make the connection between sensing the manifestation of the Holy Spirit and the experience of the gift of discerning spirits. I thought this gift was limited to sensing good and evil spirits.

Now, to each one, the manifestation of the Spirit is given for the common good.

To one, there is given through the Spirit a message of wisdom, to another a message of knowledge by means of the same Spirit ...to another distinguishing between spirits...

(1 Corinthians 12:7-10, NIV)

The Holy Spirit began to reveal to me when a person in my presence is operating through a human spirit, the Holy Spirit, or a demonic spirit. I recall when a woman in the church, Carolyn, reached out to me. The Holy Spirit spoke to me while I was in her presence. Immediately, I became aware that there was an evil spirit in my midst. I was so confounded because Carolyn was the type of person who quoted Bible verses consistently. I could not believe what the Holy Spirit had shown me. For the first time, He revealed that sometimes people will speak the words in the Bible, but their heart is not in it. Isaiah 29:13 says, *"These people come near to me with their mouth and honor me with their lips, but their hearts are far from me."* My experience with Carolyn contrasted the desires I had for the women in my presence and under my influence. I yearn for those in my presence to not only learn the Word, not just memorize the Word, but to live the Word. I was so disheartened by the presence of this spirit that I asked the Holy Spirit, "Why did you show this to me? Why would you want me to see this?"

This would not be the last time the Holy Spirit allowed me to discern the presence of other spirits. He also showed me that a person can speak words, His Word, and not be filled with His Spirit or an evil spirit. Their spirit may be the human spirit. I prayed for a young lady in church. When I placed my arms around her, when I prayed for her, I did not feel the Holy Spirit's presence. My heart did not race. I did not feel an overwhelming sense of emotion or any other indication that the Holy Spirit was present. I thought it was nerves or that I had done something wrong. A few days later, I had a follow-up conversation with the young lady, and once again, nothing. It was quite strange. So many times, the Holy Spirit had allowed me to see the soul of a person, to see beyond the flesh. Yet, when I was in this young lady's presence, there was nothing, and still, I sensed something—emptiness. It was just as disheartening as sensing an evil presence. I later found out the young lady had sought prayer under a false pretense. She spoke about the Lord, but His Spirit was not in her heart. Her intentions were not guided by evil. She was doing what she thought she should be doing.

I began to understand that "seeing things that other people do not see is not always pleasing. But it is a gift." I was told that once the glasses are on, once the Lord allows you to see with your spiritual eyes, there is no taking them off. The Holy Spirit allows me to see what He needs me to see in order to do the work He needs me to do. Sometimes, that means seeing things about a person that I don't want to see and bringing truth and correction to people who need it, even if it makes me uncomfortable, even when I don't feel like I'm the right person for the job.

Discerning spirits was and is not as clear-cut as evil versus good. It's much deeper than that. The Lord allows us to see a person's spirit. We need to see people with the fullness

> *I do not see the good in people. Because of the Holy Spirit, I see God in people.*

and the potential that God sees or has in store for that individual. This is the reason I am there: to prepare others for their transition from this world to the heavenly kingdom. The next best thing that God has for a person may not be here on earth. This is the thread that weaves the women together, as I've discussed them throughout this book. God has a greater purpose that will be fulfilled in His heavenly realm. The discerning of spirits is why I see God's saints. I thought this spiritual gift was one in which the Holy Spirit had yet to operate through me. Quite the contrary, discerning spirits was a gift that He had been unveiling to me all along. I do not see the good in people. Because of the Holy Spirit, I see God in people.

Chapter 5:
Praise Him In The Pit

²²And Reuben said to them, "Shed no blood; throw him into this pit here in the wilderness, but do not lay a hand on him"—that he might rescue him" --- that he might rescue him out of their hand to restore him to his father. (Genesis 37:22, ESV)

In fall 2022, I became ill with COVID. I had managed to dodge this illness for two years and was quite surprised when I received a positive test. In the initial five days, I became progressively ill (fever, chills, muscle aches, fatigue, broncho spasms, congestion, difficulty breathing, you name it). During this time, the Lord told me to go into my prayer room. This is the room in my home where I pray during the day in front of a self-prepared altar. It's the space where spiritual affirmations and inspirational scriptures are posted. In this space, I laid in bed, cut off from the world, for fourteen days until I regained the strength to rise. As I gained physical strength, the impact of being bedridden for two weeks began to take a toll on my mental health. As an active person who is constantly on the go, I began to feel frustrated and depressed. For several days, I cried thinking about all that I was unable to do because, for the first time in my life, my body would not do what I so desperately wanted and needed it to do.

To help lift my spirit, I turned on a sermon podcast. In that sermon, the minister discussed Joseph's

> *The pit is God's place of protection.*

story. He talked about Joseph being thrown into the pit. The pit was a good place. Joseph's brothers, his enemies, had intended to kill him, so the pit was really the place where God was protecting him. At that moment, I received a word from the Lord that pierced my soul, "I have placed you in the pit as a place of protection. Praise me while you're in the pit." I felt attacked. I felt that the enemy had tried to kill me. While I should have felt a sense of peace that the Lord was on my side, I only felt fear and distress that the devil was after me. It felt as if I had a dark shadow or yoke around my neck, stifling me. The devil did not get me this time, but what about next time? What happens next? I could see myself in a deep, dark hole with no way out. The hole was narrow. I felt isolated and alone, as though the Lord placed me here and left me. All I could do, I thought, was wait, to wait impatiently. Yes, I said that right. I waited impatiently until the moment the Lord was ready to pull me out of the pit. Only, He did not pull me out right away.

I began my time in the pit hyper-focused on the enemy. Why would he want to kill me? What would he try next? Would it be better if I just decided not to do the things that would cause the enemy to want to attack me in this way? During this time of reflection, I attended Bible study, and a word struck me. "You are too focused on what the enemy is trying to do. You need to focus on what God is doing." Of course, that was the key. I was so focused on the enemy trying to destroy me that I lost focus on the fact that God had saved me. He told me that He had placed me into this pit. He had thrown me into this deep, dark, narrow space so that one day, I could come out and not just be reunited but continue to be about my Father's business. At that moment, I was able to praise Him while still in the pit.

Before I fully recovered, before the depression left me before I returned to my daily duties, I stood still, and I rejoiced in the Lord even as I stood in this deep, dark place. I found a path to glorify Him even in the dark moments. Once I shifted my focus from the enemy to the Lord, I could consider the possibility that the more I pleased the Lord, the more I upset the enemy. I could consider that *although they plot against you, their evil schemes will never succeed.* (Psalm 21:11, NLT). I could walk confidently, knowing *the LORD frustrates the plans of the nations and thwarts all their schemes. But the LORD's plans stand firm forever; his intentions can never be shaken.* (Psalm 33: 10-11, NLT).

I did not realize that the women from church, my spiritual guides, would have such an important role during my time in the pit. I had lost sight of most things, God's direction for me and my connection to those around me, and I no longer sensed the Holy Spirit's presence. What was God trying to teach me? It felt like the Holy Spirit had left me. No matter how afraid I was of the Spirit operating through me, the idea of Him leaving me felt even worse. I felt alone and had begun to doubt all of my encounters with Him.

A God Who Sleeps

> [24] *Suddenly a furious storm came up on the lake, so that the waves swept over the boat. But Jesus was sleeping.* [25] *The disciples went and woke him, saying, "Lord, save us! We're going to drown!"* Matthew 8:24-25, NIV

Has there ever been a time when you felt the Lord had left you in your time of need? I would love to say that after a few days, after a few weeks, my time in the pit was over. Instead, it lingered for months. The Lord had gone silent on me. I could not hear the Lord, and I could not sense His Spirit. It made me feel alone, abandoned, forsaken. Did I do something to upset Him? When I prayed, it just felt like words. There was no response. I did not want to pray anymore. My spirit was broken. What could I do? I asked Him to tell me. I asked Him to show me. I continued to read His word, to lead His children through ministry, and yet, nothing. I felt abandoned. But my heart was still in it. Even when the Lord felt far from me, I wanted to please Him. Unexpectedly, the Spirit began to speak to me in a new manner. I began to dream.

Ms. Cherry told me I should start writing down my dreams. This would allow me to interpret what the Lord was trying to reveal to me. At the time, I had experienced three very vivid dreams. All the dreams contained the same elements—fear, running, and chasing. In two of the dreams, I was on a ship. These dreams reminded me of how God is my protector, and yet He sleeps. I am well aware that "We serve a God who neither slumbers nor sleeps." (Psalm 121:4). I was reminded of a time when the disciples were on a ship. On the ship, the disciples were afraid. They were in the midst of a storm. During the storm, during their fear, Jesus slept. And though He slept, He protected them. What did the Lord want them to learn while He slept? An old adage says, "A good teacher is silent during a test." What type of test was the Lord giving me? A test of faith? Did the Lord desire to send me a message that He would protect me? Perhaps the Lord wanted to assure me that He would protect me, knowing that following my illness, I would be fearful. After all, the last time He spoke to me, He said the pit is my place of protection. Jesus said to His disciples, "You of little faith, why are you so afraid?" (Matthew 8:26, NIV).

Perhaps I was having emotions like those of the disciples. I had allowed my circumstances to cause me to forget. Whether in a pit or in a storm, the Lord placed me there. Therefore, no matter the circumstances surrounding me, I was standing on Holy Ground.

When the Lord allows you into the spirit realm, using you in this way makes you an enemy of Satan. Prior to becoming ill, Satan knew that the Lord allowed me to discern between evil and good spirits. I knew when evil spirits were present. They could not sneak into the room without my sensing their presence. That made me a friend of God and an enemy of Satan. This resonated with me. For months, I suffered spiritually. The kind of suffering that comes from being a servant to my Lord and Savior, Jesus Christ. I asked the question, "Who am I that the enemy would want me dead?" At the time, I had not equated this with the suffering of my Master. They hated Him, and they will hate me. So many others throughout the Bible suffered for their life of service unto the Lord, and so will I.

I know that death knocked at my door. I know that I was on the enemy's hit list. But I am still here. The Lord saved me from death. *For in the day of trouble, he will keep me safe in his dwelling; he will hide me in the shelter of his sacred tent and set me high upon a rock. Then my head will be exalted above the enemies who surround me; at his sacred tent, I will sacrifice with shouts of joy; I will sing and make music to the Lord* (Psalm 27:5-6, NIV). Only, I did die. Spiritually speaking, a new me awakened. I knew that the old me had died, and a new me had been called. I know that she has an anointing on her life. I was excited to get to know me. I was excited about the people the Lord would send my way, those I would lead and influence. Titles are not necessary, just my testimonies of experience through spiritual warfare. Finally, I could walk in His light. Finally, I could call out to Him as Jehovah Rapha, *"But you, Lord my God, brought my life up from the pit."* (Jonah 2:6, NIV).

[1] I waited patiently for the Lord; he turned to me and heard my cry. [2] He lifted me out of the slimy pit, out of the mud and mire; he set my feet on a rock and gave me a firm place to stand. (Psalm 40:1-2, NIV)

Chapter 6:
My Season In The
Wilderness

*² Remember how the LORD your God led you all the way
in the wilderness these forty years, to humble and test you in
order to know what was in your heart, whether or not you
would keep his commands. (Deuteronomy 8:2 NIV)*

Spiritual Warfare? Or Test From God?

Why would the Lord need me to remain in a pit? What
did I need to be protected from? I wasn't sure if He was
testing me to see if I would still write this book, even
when I no longer heard His voice. If it wasn't a test, was
He still protecting me? Perhaps the reason I remained in
the pit was not for me. Maybe I have remained in the pit
so that I can teach others that when you make the decision
to live a Spirit-filled life, a life of faith, there will be
tribulation. I can tell them that when things become
difficult, when you go through hardships, for His
namesake, He will protect you through faith, He will see
you through. But I also had to consider the possibility that
God really did not want me to write this book.

I was just starting to understand and accept my spiritual gifts and then it felt like they were gone. Ms. Cherry said the Lord was still speaking to me, but He was doing it through my dreams. My dreams were revealing to me that the Lord would protect me. They told me that I would soon triumph over my trials and obstacles. Dreams. Why dreams? Why would the Lord stop speaking to me with a voice and begin speaking through my dreams?

I was breaking down. I was falling apart. I felt as if my prayers were going unheard. Either I was being tested by the Lord, He had allowed the devil to test me, or He trusted me enough to be silent. I questioned whether there would be a day when He would allow me to hear His voice. Jesus suffered, and our suffering makes us more like Him. Thus, my suffering would not move the Lord to speak to me. It was not going to make Him any more empathetic to my situation. He knows there will be times when we must suffer. But I wondered why the Lord would show me hidden things and then take this gift from me. Was He angry with me? What did He want from me? What did He want me to do? I had so many questions but so few answers.

During this time, I wondered, "Where are all the people?" Where are the people, indeed? The ones who said, "I'll pray for you," but did not pray. The ones who said, "Call me if you need me," but did not answer, call, or text me back. I needed those people. I needed those people on days when I felt overwhelmed and drained — mentally, emotionally, and spiritually. I needed these people on days when we had to visit the oncologist. I recall the day when we were given the treatment plans for my husband. Eight weeks, they said. My husband and I would have to drive a total of four hours every day for eight weeks so that he could receive radiation treatment. I knew the Lord was with me, but it did not feel that way. I did not hear Him. I did not feel His presence. But I knew He was with me, even when it hurt. God had broken me to a point where I had no option but to trust Him. Maybe that was the point. It seemed that I could not call on other people to help me get through this season of my life. I appreciated the brief check-ins from the women's ministry at church, but they never filled the void or removed the ache I felt through this season. Without His voice, without His Spirit, without family and friends to call on, I had no choice but to trust that God (the Father) had His reasons and plans that required me to experience this kind of testing — this kind of training. It had been easy for me to follow the Holy Spirit's instruction when I could hear His voice clearly. How do you follow God during times of trial when you no longer hear His voice?

A Test Of Faith

When God didn't speak to me (well, when I thought He had stopped speaking to me), it was not because He had left me. I had not done anything wrong. I had not done anything to deserve the tribulations coming my way. I asked, "Lord, what is that you want me to do for you?" I had the wrong thought process. Doing good for others and serving the Lord did not exempt me from struggle or tribulation. That was lesson one. The next lesson I learned was that God was not seeking for me to do something for Him. Instead, He wanted to teach me. He wanted me to learn. During this time of reflection, I attended a noon-day Bible study session at my church. An older gentleman was attending Elder Hall. He told me his testimony of a time when the Lord took him through a faith test. It was a conversation he had with the Lord. He likened it to a math test.

The Lord asked Elder Hall, "When a math teacher gives you a problem to solve, does the math teacher know the answer?" Elder Hall responded, "Yes, he knows." Then the Lord replied, "Even though the math teacher knows the answer, he gives you the problem anyway, and he asks you to solve it." Elder Hall replied, "That's correct." The Lord then said, "So then, the teacher does not give you the problem because he needs the answer; he gives you the problem to teach you as the answer is revealed."

This teaching was so critical for spiritual growth and maturity. I have observed that when we begin to learn God's Word, we are eager to share it with others, to offer guidance during times of need, and to bring salvation to others. But, if we move too quickly, we run the risk of depleting ourselves. It's essential to allow God to make spiritual deposits within us and continue to consult the Holy Spirit to receive ongoing guidance. Subsequently, when God sends us to encourage others and be His mouthpiece, we have something to give and still have the spiritual fortitude to continue to run our personal race. I am reminded of Paul's advice to the Corinthians. *"I strike a blow to my body and make it my slave so that after I have preached to others, I myself will not be disqualified for the prize."* (1 Corinthians 9:27, NIV). It is important that as we teach and guide others, we do not run out of energy and mental fortitude to run the personal race the Lord has set for us.

God is Silent, and Yet He Speaks

For months, I had gone without hearing a word from the Lord. I had gone without hearing His voice. I felt like giving up on seeking for the Lord to speak to me. In my former years, I had recognized the Lord's voice, and yet the Holy Spirit still guided me. But once the Lord spoke to me, after He unveiled a new world to me, it was difficult to go back. How do you return to a life where you don't hear Him speaking aloud?

The Lord also had not been restored by spiritual perception. For five months, I did not sense the Holy Spirit's presence. That feeling I once described of being "overcome" and filled with the Spirit was gone. What did this mean? Would it return? I prayed consistently that it would return, that He would return to me. Without it, I did not know how to guide the women. It was like driving with a cloudy windshield. I could still drive, but I could not see anything. So, I just drove, praying that I was headed in the right direction. Once again, I spoke to Mother Evelyn about growing weary of being faced with issue after issue, problem after problem. Even more challenging was dealing with these issues during the time when I thought the Lord had stopped speaking to me. She described it as "hell." She said when God speaks to you and shows hidden things, going without it can feel like hell until it returns.

During this time, I gave Dr. Enola a journal entry I had written titled, *The Water is God*. I felt the urge to give these words to her. It was to inspire her to write a poem. Dr. Enola asked how I knew she needed it. Quite the contrary, I did not know that she needed a word of inspiration. But, through this interaction, I was reminded that even when we don't hear His voice when we think God has gone silent, He speaks. I was reminded that His Spirit lives and breathes within me. It is the Holy Spirit who intercedes and communicates with God on our behalf. So then, it only made sense that God would communicate with me through the Spirit in a language that only the Spirit understands. In times when we feel we "just know," it is a sign that the Holy Spirit has received a word, and so God speaks through His Spirit.

While I was comforted in knowing the Spirit was still speaking. I yearned to hear His voice again, to hear a direct message, to see with my spiritual eyes. But, if His voice had not left me, I would not have learned a valuable lesson. God speaks to us in and through His silence. I had accepted that I could return to this world that I once knew, a world where I did not sense Him or feel His presence, and yet a world where His Spirit still guides me. Even in His silence, my God speaks!

Ears to Hear

I have come to realize that the Holy Spirit speaks in many ways. The problem was not that the Lord had stopped speaking. The problem was I had not learned the different ways of listening. What had I learned? That the Lord will plant a thought in our mind, send a mental picture of someone He seeks to send a message, He will send me to a Bible scripture that I never intended to read or guide me to a sermon that feels as if it was purposed for me. He will plant the seed in a dream that requires interpretation. Some of these methods of speaking were new to me, but for others, I simply needed to be reminded of all of the ways the Spirit had spoken to me in the past.

If God speaks in *diverse* ways, and the Bible tells us He does, then we need to be prepared to listen in *diverse* ways. We have been taught to listen with our ears, and we communicate with body language and written language. When the Holy Spirit gives instruction, it's our time to listen; it's our time to trust. God did not speak to Noah every day. He gave him instructions to build the ark and trusted him to complete the task he was given. Nehemiah did not hear from the Lord each day, but he focused on the last instruction he was given to build the wall. God did not speak to Solomon daily. And yet, He used David to provide him instructions, "Build the temple." We must continue to progress and move forward with the instructions we are given. We must trust that if the Lord has not chimed in with a new instruction, His expectation is that we continue to do the last thing He asked us to do.

Think about your GPS or navigation system as analogous to following instructions. The GPS has moments when it does not speak. In fact, the GPS waits until it's near time for us to take action to offer new instructions. Until the appointed time comes, we are to stay on the path and continue to do the last thing we were instructed to do. Trust that when the timing is right, the Holy Spirit will speak. Instructions will come. Trust that during this time of what feels like silence, when the road gets bumpy, when there are traffic jams, when you get tired of driving, this is the time to keep moving. Those who stay the course will receive new instruction and the gifts that await all who believe, even in moments of silence.

Chapter 7:
The Call To Ministry

Who Does He Say I Am?

One evening, I was in bed watching a television program when my prayer alarm went off. I got up to pray, and I asked the Lord, "Who am I? What is my calling? Why was I placed on this earth?" When I returned to my television program, one of the characters (in what felt like a very random statement) said, "The salt of the earth." This was not a religious movie. Was God answering me? Mother Evelyn had previously told me that oftentimes when she asks the Lord a question, someone on the television answers the question. What does it mean to be the salt of the earth? To be called to influence others, go wherever God chooses to send me, exalt His name, teach doctrine, and bring salvation to others. Is this my purpose, my calling? Jesus referred to His disciples as the salt of the earth. They were persecuted for righteousness' sake. It comes with the territory of doing God's work. I knew that I wanted to walk in this purpose, but I did not know what the Lord wanted me to do. I did not feel supported or guided. I just felt that I was wandering, lost, without direction. Little did I know that was about to change.

Evangelist/Missionary

In fall 2022, my church had an ordination service. My pastor wanted to ordain his ministry leaders. I was ordained as an Evangelist/Missionary. This was a peculiar time in my life. I remained in what I have referred to as my time in the pit. Internally, I had been struggling, unable to hear God's voice, unable to sense His Spirit. Yet, I was growing in the ministry. This was a role that I had not previously considered. Instead of seeking a role among the ministers, it was happening to me.

I realized what the Lord meant when He said He would protect me. Although I had been called by the Lord, I was still very much in seed form. I was still vulnerable in my spiritual walk. When the enemy was unable to destroy me with COVID, it felt like he tried to attack me through my husband. My husband, however, is a man with the spiritual gift of faith. It was quickly apparent that if the enemy was going to use my husband to attempt to get me, it would be through the testing of my faith. Could I trust God when I could not hear Him? Could I commit myself to the work of a ministry leader without the spiritual perception I once had?

During this time, I attended a ministry class offered by my church. The pastor required us to create a five-minute sermonette to be delivered to the church congregation. Ironically, the topic the Holy Spirit gave me was *Hope*. I was excited. I had two streams of thought for the message, "Get your hopes up" and "The Profanity of Hopelessness." However, once I received the news of my husband's diagnosis, I felt that I could no longer speak a word on hope. How could God ask me to edify others with a message of encouragement and hope when I felt hopeless? Maybe that was the point. The Holy Spirit wanted me to speak a message on the importance of hope and faith, but more importantly, He wanted me to do it from a place of experience, a testimony of how He showed me that He is the God of Hope. After all, *"faith is the substance of things **hoped for**..."* (Hebrews 11:1, NIV, emphasis added).

There was a part of me that honestly believed my husband did not have cancer. If I just believed that he was cancer-free, the miraculous would happen. That was not the case. And yet, that was not the worst part of my experience. This occurred during this time when I no longer sensed the Holy Spirit. How could I continue writing this book if I did not feel connected to the Holy Spirit? I had so many questions. Will my husband be healed from cancer? Will I become a mother? Will I once again receive a prophetic word? Will the Holy Spirit send me another vision? The Lord says *I will never leave you nor forsake you*. Yet, that is how I felt...that the Lord had left me and had now forsaken me. How could I write an inspirational message on hope when I felt utterly hopeless?

My Calling Challenged

Soon after being ordained, the devil tried to tempt me. I recognized that having the title of Evangelist in the church is an honor

12 Rejoice and be glad, because great is your reward in heaven, for in the same way they persecuted the prophets who were before you. 13 You are the salt of the earth. (Matthew 5:12-13, NIV)

and that not all are called to evangelize. I was placed in a position where I was asked to pray due to my evangelist title. It felt very condescending, especially since the individual first referred to me as a deacon. I pray often, both privately and publicly. While it would have been no problem for me to pray, it was as though I was being called out to prove myself. "Well, she's a deacon; let the deacon pray." Shortly after this moment, my calling as an evangelist came into question. I was told by someone close to me that they were surprised that I became an evangelist, considering that I had not attended church regularly as a child. They also said that while they saw me having a successful future while growing up, this (getting ordained) was not something they saw coming. The question then arose if this was something that the Holy Spirit had called me to or if it was something I had decided to do on my own. Wow. Words do hurt, especially when they come from those who are closest to you.

Whatever I am called to do is a conversation between the Holy Spirit and me. I do not need man's approval. In that moment, I was reminded that Paul's calling from the Lord was challenged by others. *"But when God, who set me apart from my mother's womb and called me by his grace, was pleased to reveal his son in me so that I might preach him among the Gentiles, my immediate response was not to consult any human being."* (Galatians, 1:15 NIV). I was comforted by God's words on allowing other people to challenge who He has called me to be. In the book of Isaiah, the Lord says that you allow mere mortals to make you worry because you forget who your creator is (Isaiah 51:12). We often forget that we were created and that we were created for a purpose. No man or woman has the power to change the calling for which God has anointed us. Yet, we allow people to speak words into us, to make us doubt who God created us to be. I admit that I doubted the anointing that God placed on my life. I doubted the purpose for which I was created. It was never my intention to be in a position to bring God to others. Sometimes, our actions result in a "make God laugh" moment.

The Guilt In Spreading The Good News

As an evangelist, one who spreads the good news of God's grace for the purpose of salvation, I take joy in the thought of others coming into intimacy with our

Heavenly Father and with His Spirit. It brings me great pleasure to bear witness to the spiritual growth of others and watch them blossom before my eyes. There should be no shame or guilt in bringing the word of God to others. And yet, there are times when I struggle with watching someone else's spiritual growth. It's easy to observe the positive impact and the connection with God that results from spiritual growth. Who wouldn't love to see this?! The challenge, however, is that I recognize when someone makes the decision to live a Christlike life, struggle and trials await them. I observed this in a woman from our women's ministry at church, Ms. Krystle. She has attended the church almost since its inception. Ms. Krystle attends Bible study weekly and serves in church consistently. Even at her tender age, which is in her late 60s, she had not established a relationship with the Word of God. She had not come to understand the Word in a way that would allow her to have an intimate relationship with God and His Holy Spirit.

I began to speak words of encouragement to Ms. Krystle. When the Lord gave me a word for her, I was obedient. I shared it with her. Most importantly, when she was afraid to step into her calling, I was there for her, uplifting her so that her fear of judgment would not keep her from her purpose and all that God had in store for her. I watched Ms. Krystle come out of her shell, her cocoon. Slowly but surely, I began to coach her through her calling. Ms. Krystle began to facilitate our prayer calls, read scriptures aloud, and even attended our church's ministry class. It was in the ministry class that the enemy tried to stifle Ms. Krystle. He tried to hold her hostage to a spirit of fear and bashfulness. One night, Ms. Krystle was assigned to explain a leadership principle in class. She tried to get out of it. I encouraged her to explain it just as we had discussed. Though apprehensive, she went on to explain. I knew that by doing this, Ms. Krystle had taken a step of faith and a swipe against the enemy. We don't consider this part. The more we step out on faith, the bigger our faith steps, and the greater the disruption in the enemy's plans. The enemy would accept no other option than to attempt to pull her back.

Over time, Ms. Krystle began to face a season of trials. These trials felt random. For example, she hit a deer, was pulled over by the police in a traffic stop and began to have several minor health problems. Ms. Krystle cried out, feeling like she was under attack. Indeed, she was. I was not surprised by the enemy's actions. Ms. Krystle was beginning to recognize who she was in Christ. While that was good news for her, it was bad news for Satan. I knew he would have no other choice but to try to break her confidence and to break her spirit. But I also knew that because of her acts of faith and her good deeds, Ms. Krystle was in great hands. Although she felt attacked, the Lord was on her side, and surely, He wouldn't even allow her to *hurt her foot on a stone*. So, what was the problem? My human nature felt guilty.

By helping Ms. Krystle read the Bible and encouraging her through the fear, she would now join in the struggles of those of us who live a life in the Spirit. I do not want those under my influence to experience hardships. The thought of it is utterly heartbreaking. And yet, I am comforted knowing that the enemy strikes against those he perceives to be a threat. Ms. Krystle had transitioned from being a shy caterpillar who was wrapped in the Lord's embrace like a cocoon and has now blossomed into a butterfly. This is my hope for all those the Holy Spirit calls me to influence. They are my caterpillars, and there is no shame in my hope that they will come into the Lord's embrace like cocoons and one day be revealed as new creatures. Galatians 6:2 tells us to "Carry each other's burdens, and in this way, *you will fulfill the law of Christ.*" Knowing that those who live in the faith will face trials, the Lord has positioned me to be there for them, offer comfort and support, and encourage others, even when it's tough for me to witness. Just as I remind them that blessings are on the way, I must remind myself to remain focused on the blessings that are to come from their salvation.

A Time Such as This

Many great spiritual leaders describe how some of their worst life experiences occurred during a time when they were being thrust into the spotlight. God used them to speak to His people, and yet, behind the scenes, they were experiencing *the Word the Lord put forth*. For me, that was a message of hope: *Hope While it Hurts*. "Five Minutes to Encourage One Another"- That was the title of my message. Sunday, January 29, 2023. I thank God for this day. I stood in the pulpit for the first time and gave a message of encouragement. It felt amazing. For years, I asked God why He requested that I do more. Why must I read more or study more? Why do I always have to be the bigger person? Why do you constantly ask me to turn the other cheek? Why must I be above reproach? When I stepped down from the pulpit, I realized that all these years, God had asked me to hold myself to a higher standard so that one day, I could grace His pulpit. In that moment, I did not know where God was leading me, but I knew that if He was going to use me to teach His people, I needed to carry myself with love, to be kind to those who were not kind to me, to have a pure heart and clean hands, to be noble, to be honorable, and to be true. If I were never again to be given the opportunity to speak in front of a congregation, in that moment, it all made sense. I felt that all the Lord had asked me to do, all that He had asked me to go through, was for "a time such as this."

The Voice, He Gave Me

One of the difficulties of speaking the Word in front of a church congregation is my voice. I do not speak very loudly. Over the years, people have commented that my voice sounds like a radio broadcaster, while others describe it as soothing or comforting. The point is that I do not have the typical preacher or minister's voice. I am a professor. That is what I do, profess. My voice is not loud. It isn't boisterous. *Poignant* is a word that is often used to describe the tone of voice. Why am I describing this? Knowing who you are and your identity in Christ is essential to doing His work. More important is embracing that He created you to be this way for a purpose and on purpose. When I get into a spirit of comparison, I remind myself that when I prefer someone else's traits or gifts over mine, in a way, I am telling God that I do not like His creation. With wisdom beyond our understanding, the Lord knows that no single one of us can reach all of us. Therefore, He molds us so that we may reach someone, even one, whom others cannot reach. With this in mind, I have embraced the gentle, poignant voice the Lord intentionally gave me, the voice He created just for me. I submitted to offering my voice for the Lord to reach His sheep, even for the one sheep that has been lost. My voice may not be the loud voice in the crowd, or the voice the congregation is accustomed to hearing, or the voice that reaches the masses. But this voice is uniquely mine. It is the voice God, my creator, made especially for me.

Shiloh

Previously, I mentioned that the Prophet Samuel had meaning in my life. I reside at 113 Shiloh. Some languages define *Shiloh* as "peace." Others suggest that it means "he who is sent." One translation says it means "His gift." I was inspired to take a look at the book of Samuel to find 113. 1 Samuel 1:3 states, *"Year after year this man went up from his town to worship and sacrifice to the Lord Almighty at Shiloh, where Hophini and Phineas, the two sons of Eli, were priests of the Lord."* I believe God has purposed me to be here, in this place, on this street, in this home, at this time. In Samuel, Shiloh is the location where the priest lives. I could simply say that this was a coincidence or that I was overthinking the situation. But I believe that God places people exactly where they need to be, and, at the moment, they need to be there. I am reminded of the story of Saul being blinded on the road to Damascus. God was working behind the scenes to ensure that Ananias would meet Saul at a designated location. This was not by happenstance.

I met a young lady at Bible study. It was not a day when I typically attended Bible study. As God would have it, the young lady had delivered groceries to my home earlier that morning. I did not see her during the delivery. When I walked into Bible study, I told her my name, and she recalled it from the order. She then proceeded to tell everyone how she had been blessed by my home and presence. The young lady was at a place where the Holy Spirit had called her to Shiloh. The emotion of feeling that He wanted her to arrive on a street that meant *peace,* then to arrive at the church and see that the resident of that home was not only a God-fearing woman but a member of her new church. To God be the glory. It was a blessing for her, but this moment was a blessing for me as well. It was a reminder from the Holy Spirit about where I live, this intentional place He brought me to, and a reminder of who I am in Him.

Shiloh is the place God brought me to. It is the place where I first heard the Lord speak to me in an audible voice. It is the place where He told me to create the prayer line and to refer to it as *The Tabernacle.* The place where He would come to us and where His presence would always be in the midst. Shiloh is the place where I received the mantle of ministry, the mantle of teaching God's Word. Yet, it seemed that I had pieces to a puzzle, but a few were still missing. I believed the Lord was sending me a message. If spiritually, I represent the priest, what does God want me to do? Perhaps He doesn't want me to do anything. Maybe He just wants me to know who I am, who I am in His eyes. Maybe He created me to be a minister at heart. I had many questions. I have been told not to ask questions but to seek God. Honestly, at some point in our spiritual journey, we all have questions. It's a sign that we are growing spiritually. It's a natural part of growing. The questions, however, are not for us to answer on our own. They are for us to consult the Holy Spirit. Only then will we receive the answers He wants us to reveal.

Chapter 8:
Called But Still In A
Growing Season

But the seed falling on good soil refers to someone who hears the word and understands it. This is the one who produces a crop, yielding a hundred, sixty or thirty times what was sown." (Matthew 13:23 NIV)

I liken my progression into ministry to growing a garden. Many biblical truths are rooted in the concept of gardening—growing something from seed form to harvest. At this stage in my life, the seed of a minister has been planted. I am in a space where I know God has called me, but I have yet to reach my harvest season. I am in good company. David was told he would be king, and then he went back to the sheep pen (1 Samuel 16:12-13). Joseph dreamed that his family would bow to him and then was thrown into the pit (Genesis 37). Two things can be true: I can be called and yet still have not arrived. I thought that by the time I finished this book, I would have "arrived." I thought that I would be in the place and space where all that God had been training me for would have come to fruition. The truth is, no matter where I am on this journey, I am exactly where God wants me to be.

David was aware of his calling to become king long before it ever happened. Instead of focusing on becoming king, he focused on serving. That is what God has asked me to do. Not to focus on who He has called me to be. Not to focus on who He has anointed me to be. Instead, the Lord has given me a gift. The gift of knowing that He has anointed me. He has called me for an appointed time. Instead of trying to figure out the final piece of the puzzle to my calling, my purpose is just to serve, knowing that the time will come. That is all I need to know. In the meantime, I am focusing on serving in whatever capacity He calls me to.

In the summer, I grow a garden. Gardening is an activity that allows me to see God's handiwork in action. I am able to witness the potential to grow and subsequently grow. As a teacher, I observe potential in others. I am in a position to, figuratively, plant seeds and watch them grow. The seeds are planted in good soil. The seeds grow into seedlings. When it is time for me to transplant, not all of my seedlings make it. The environment destroys some of them. I am constantly competing with other living creatures that want to devour my plants before they can make it to the harvest stage. As the gardener, I know these battles are coming.

It's my job not to expose my seedlings to the elements before they are ready. I cannot know exactly when they are ready until I test them. When the seedlings have grown, I take them outside and expose them to the elements (i.e., the sun, wind, and rain) for a few hours per day to see how they will respond. None of them respond well the first few times so I bring them back in. I expect this. Once I see that they are strong enough to withstand the elements, I transplant them so that they can begin a new stage in the growth process.

The stages of growth for a seed are true of us as well. A seed is planted in us. The seed will grow. Initially, we cannot see the growth, but if we are good soil, the seed will soon break open and begin to mature. Which of these will mature enough to bear fruit? Some of my seeds will allow life's circumstances to weaken them. Some will try to produce fruit before it's their time. When the seedlings produce too soon, they produce bad fruit. Unfortunately, this can be just as bad as not producing any fruit at all. The plants have roots and the nutrients to produce fruit, but they do not have enough deposited into them to sustain both themselves and the fruit.

Once the plant produces fruit or vegetables that reach their full maturity, they can be harvested. At the end of the journey, the harvest has two tasks: to produce new seeds and to fill others. The plant's job is to maintain. While it may be difficult to maintain, the process of reaching this stage is critical. The plants are rooted. They have received enough nutrients to not only produce good fruit but be sustained in the process. I see this so often in my students and in the church. People receive milk but are still in infancy. They rush out into the world, anxious to teach the lessons newly learned, only to be choked by premature exposure to the elements of this world. How does Mark describe it?

> [18]*Still others, like seed sown among thorns, hear the word;* [19]*but the worries of this life, the deceitfulness of wealth, and the desires for other things come in and choke the word, making it unfruitful* (Mark 4:18-19, NIV).

Growing in the Spirit takes time, but it's for a good reason. If we are in a hurry to release what has been deposited in us, we will never reach our potential to sustain all that is being placed within us. We will never grow to bear fruit that will ultimately bear fruit (Galatians 5:22-23).

The gift we receive from the Holy Spirit is a seed that transforms from immaturity to maturity through stages of growth. The process feels slow and, at times, painful. But this process of progressing from immaturity to maturity in Christ is the time when we need to be present and patient. It is not the time to try to skip to the end. It is natural to become anxious. In the past, I have been anxious. I wanted to know what my purpose was, what God had in store for me, and who He created me to be. Instead of focusing on what was to come, I needed to focus on what was and what is. Whatever our now is, it is the perfect time to embrace and appreciate the moment.

When we are growing, and our spiritual gifts are being cultivated, there is a tendency to desire to share all that the Holy Spirit has taught us. It's important to remember the analogy of the seed. When my seedlings began to grow, I tested them by exposing them to outside elements. While we are babes and spiritually immature, God exposes us to small tests. Then He brings us back in. For me, this was a time when I recognized the Holy Spirit working through me. It was a time when I began to recognize my spiritual gifts. Shortly after, I noticed that as I endured trials, those spiritual gifts were not as present, still present, but lying dormant until the Spirit was ready to use them. God was testing me. The tests became longer, more severe, and more complicated. Throughout this process, I became stronger. I was stronger in my faith, stronger in my ability to persevere, and stronger in spiritual discernment.

As God recognized my strength and realized that I had become rooted in His Word, the assignments escalated. I would love to say that during this time, my spiritual gifts grew. That was not the case. By passing the test, the Spirit realized He could use me. That meant He could use the gifts He had placed within me. The Holy Spirit placed me into positions to teach His Word, to teach His people, and to offer guidance and encouragement. It was critical for me to wait for God to bring these opportunities to me. I now bared the fruit (love, joy, peace, patience, kindness, goodness, faithfulness, gentleness, and self-control) to offer others. However, if I had gone out on my own without realizing God's *kairos* time, then just like the seedlings, I would have produced fruit prematurely. I needed to wait for God to build up my roots, to build a solid foundation within me. By waiting, when I am now sent to help others, I have a sufficient deposit from His Spirit to share Him with others and still have the capacity to battle my personal spiritual warfare. I have observed others who immediately release what God has recently deposited into them. Without those roots, they are vulnerable to being broken, delaying their growth, or being overtaken by whatever circumstances life brings their way. God wants us to be plentiful. He wants us to bear fruit and share His Spirit as He has shared Him with us. But He also wants us to be sustained, and that takes time.

I realized that I had been called by God the moment I recognized that His Spirit had been planted and was growing within me like a seed. The seed was alive and present but still needed time to grow from an idea (seed form) to immaturity (seedling) to a plant (maturity) capable of both producing and bearing good fruit. Even at this moment, I am embracing the fact that He has called me, and yet, it is for an appointed time. The gifts and fruit of the Spirit go hand in hand. The goal is not to learn about your gifts and then set out to use them. No. The goal is to mature in character and to mature in Christ so that you may become fruitful. When the fruits of your character begin to appear—love, joy, peace, patience, kindness, goodness, faithfulness, gentleness, and self-control; you won't need to learn how to best use your gifts because His Holy Spirit will do the work. He will use you to complete His Mighty Works.

Chapter 9:
We Are But Clay

²⁴ Then Jesus said to his disciples, "Whoever wants to be my disciple must deny themselves and take up their cross and follow me. (Matthew 16:24 NIV)

Revelation required letting go of me. We cannot be God's vessel and have our own agenda. Using His gifts requires complete surrender to His purpose for me and my path in life. Only God knows the true reason why each of us was created. When I was born, the Lord had a specific plan in mind for me. He knew the experiences I needed as a child that would allow me to grow into the person He called me to be. Not only did He know how those experiences would impact me, but how I could use those experiences to impact the lives of others. He knew my physical features and personality characteristics long before I was in my mother's womb. He knew which features would allow me to bring His Word to His people and the imperfect features that would make me humble.

For years, I fought with the idea of becoming a professor. I did not want to teach. I was trained to conduct research. I saw myself as a researcher. Fast-forward, I became a professor. I was having yet another "make God laugh" moment. When I reflect on my life over the years, I see that I have always been placed in a position to teach others. In my first job out of college, I assisted my colleagues in learning new technology. I was always good at explaining concepts and instructions to other people. I never thought about this as teaching others. If I'm honest, it was as though God was preparing me for my future role of becoming a teacher. Yet not in the traditional sense of teaching. Little did I know He was preparing me to become a teacher for His kingdom.

When I began teaching as a professor, I was frustrated. But I decided that instead of being frustrated, I would submit to God's plan for my life. It was apparent that He wanted me to teach, that I had been created to teach. The Lord had brought me so far in life. I had a lot to be thankful for. I grew up in project housing with a single mom. My dad had a drug addiction while I was growing up. By all intents and purposes, earning a doctorate and becoming a professor was a path that only God could have forged. Instead of complaining about my teaching role, I decided to use my teaching as a way to say "Thank you" to God for all that He had done for me and for all He had brought me through. I turned teaching into my service unto the Lord.

How often do we pay attention to our skills and our natural talents and consider how they might be used to reach God's people? I had not considered that the things I was naturally good at were not created in me for my benefit. Our talents and gifts were not meant to be kept to ourselves but to edify God's people. My talent for communicating and explaining information was not a gift designed for my professional life that happened to benefit the church. It was quite the opposite. God created me with a gift to teach in the church and for ministry. My career and professional life benefits from that gift.

Motivational Gifts

When we are first saved, we are given spiritual gifts. I like to think of these gifts as God's motivation for creating us.

We have different gifts, according to the grace given to each of us. (Romans 12:6-8.)

Better said, "What gifts has God placed in you that will allow you to motivate His people?" The Bible describes seven motivational gifts: prophecy, service, teaching, exhortation, giving, administration, and mercy (Romans 12:6-8). When God created us, He placed in us the tools for edifying. Not for our personal edification but to bring praise and joy to Him and to bring salvation to His people. How can these gifts be used to help you motivate God's sheep? The Bible tells us that the Lord made us in His image and likeness. His personality traits have been implanted in us. In our daily lives and busy schedules, it's easy to forget that we have Christ in us.

God created me to be a teacher and an encourager. These were traits of my character long before I ever recognized them. In fact, these were traits that others saw in me long before I recognized them. Helping people and explaining complicated information in its simplest form were things that I always had a talent for. Most importantly, I recognized that though I can be impatient and a perfectionist in my daily life when teaching others and assisting them in thinking through a problem, I become patient. If someone were to observe my actions throughout the day, they would likely find that I have the most patience while I am teaching. I am not easily irritated or annoyed by the idea of questions or new learners.

It's important to know which motivational gifts God has given us. God created us with these gifts in mind. God created me with specific gifts in mind. Yet, my spiritual journey required me to reflect on how those gifts manifested over the years. Many of our motivational gifts may be identified in hindsight by thinking back on the ways God has used us over the years. When I first started out as a professor, I knew that I was good at it, but I didn't have a passion for it. I enjoyed interacting with the students. I enjoyed mentoring them.

The students also pushed me to be vulnerable in a way that I had not expected. When I started my position, the students would knock at my office door frequently. They wanted guidance, but not for coursework. Many students wanted to talk about life. At that point in my personal life, I was someone with many walls up. I was not interested in becoming a "counselor." I recall thinking that I had the wrong mindset about teaching. The Lord had brought me so far in life. I felt that even if I did not enjoy being an educator, I owed God. That's how I realized the gift He gave me for teaching. I went to work each day with an "I owe God" mentality. As a way of giving to the Lord, I teach and exhort wherever He calls me to.

Prophecy

While teaching and exhorting were gifts that I was comfortable with, I struggled with other ways the Holy Spirit had decided to use me. I struggled with the spiritual gift of prophecy. In fact, it's the spiritual gift I struggled with the most. I questioned if an implanted word or image were really my thoughts. I feared how people would respond if I gave them a message from the Lord. Who am I to be in a position to bring a message from God to others? When describing prophecy to others, the concept of rain seems to be an appropriate analogy.

You and another person are in the house. You realize it's raining outside, but the other person does not. It's not clear how you know it's raining. You don't see it, and you don't hear it,

114

but you know. Deep down, there is an awareness of things your physical senses cannot detect. You don't see it, can't hear it, you don't feel or smell it. The other person is headed outside. Do you warn them that it's raining? Not everyone will appreciate your warning to them. Some people will not trust you. They will say that it's not raining just because you say it's raining. Others, however, will be appreciative and will take heed of your advice. They will prepare themselves to go out into the rain. You cannot allow the few people who don't believe in stopping you from warning others.

This analogy seems so simple—it's raining! Who doesn't want to be warned that it's raining outside? Likewise, why would we ever be afraid to tell someone it's raining outside? It's important that we don't decide who we give God's Word based on how we perceive they will respond. If a person decides to go outside in the rain, it shouldn't be because we made the decision not to tell them it's raining.

When I speak of rain, this concept is easy. It's silly not to warn someone that it's raining, especially when you can prevent them from getting wet. When the subject is prophecy, we make it more complicated than this. I made it more complicated than it was. Sure, not everyone will believe me. The belief, however, starts with me. If I'm not convinced that God is speaking to me, why should anyone else? The act of sharing a prophetic word is not about the recipient's response to the information.

Communicating the message is about my obedience to the Holy Spirit's instruction. He has given us instructions that will help someone, protect them, and encourage them. God has entrusted us with information. He seeks to deliver His message, His Word, to His people. It's uncomfortable, at least; it is for me. It's difficult to make sense of it. However, not making use of this precious information is selfish in many ways. Why would the Holy Spirit allow you to keep His gift if you are not going to be fruitful with it?

When I first experienced spiritual gifts, I wanted them to have a name. I wanted to place a label on how the Holy Spirit was manifesting through me. I wanted to answer the question, "Who am I?" A seer or a discerner? Am I a prophet or an evangelist? A teacher or a minister? Did God create me to be all of these things, working in concert to encourage others? I recognized that the Holy Spirit was operating through me in many ways. But most important was acknowledging that this was not the right way to approach the gifts of the Spirit. I was asking the wrong questions. The Holy Spirit does not bring us gifts to give us a title, a position, or a supernatural power. The gifts serve a purpose. They are designed to edify, teach, correct, bring salvation to others, and reveal God's kingdom. The title I hold is "Available." I am merely *Available* to God's Spirit using me. Am I available to do His work? Am I available to teach His people? Am I available to feed His sheep? Those are the questions I now ask myself. If today the Lord calls me to be an Exhorter, then I'm an Exhorter. If He calls me to be an Evangelist, then I'm an Evangelist. The point is that the Lord calls us to serve in various capacities. No matter the role, on any given day, we simply need to be willing and ready to serve.

Chapter 10:
Out Of The Pit, Into The
Promise

¹Be careful to follow every command I am giving you today, so that you may live and increase and may enter and possess the land the Lord promised on oath to your ancestors ² Remember how the Lord your God led you all the way in the wilderness these forty years, to humble and test you in order to know what was in your heart, whether or not you would keep his commands.
(Deuteronomy 8:1-2, NIV)

One morning, I began my devotion as I normally do. On this particular morning, instead of opening the Bible to the next chapter, I allowed the Bible to fall open. My prayer is, "Lord, what would you like to say to me this morning?" The Bible opened to Deuteronomy 8. The subject, *Out of the Wilderness*. It had been nearly a year since God sent me the message that He was sending me into a pit. The pit was my place of protection. It seemed that the Lord was telling me that the time had come for Him to bring me out of the pit and into the promise. At that point, I had only contemplated why God felt the need to protect me. I thought that there must be danger or even that the enemy was coming after me. But when I received the message that I was coming out, I began to reflect on my time in the pit.

When I entered the pit, I was weak. My body was healing from being ill. I was entering my roles within the church as a teacher, evangelist, and as a missionary. I was surrounded by others, yet I felt isolated. The trials I was up against were challenges I could not face with other people. I had to face them with the Holy Spirit. He was the only person who could bring me peace while in the pit. It was a time of growth, reflection, and development. We see many examples of this process in the Bible. People are sent through the wilderness, thrown into pits, and locked in dens. These deep, dark places, while intended for harm, become places where those who dwell can focus on the Lord. A place where we have no choice but to focus on the Lord. He shows us examples of this in our daily lives. The transformations that only occur in the dark and when we are isolated. Butterflies emerge after the caterpillar transforms into a deep, dark cocoon. The creature that goes in does not look or behave like the new creature that emerges. An image is captured on film only to be processed in the dark. Out of the darkness, an image of what was once hidden but had not been developed soon emerges from the dark with a clear image of what needs to be revealed. If the butterfly or image leaves their dark place too soon or prematurely, they will never see the promise that God has in store for them.

As I prepared to emerge from my pit, I spoke with Dr. Enola about our calling in the ministry. She suggested that her gifts represented the Lord's hands. An important part of her ministry is to give to others. Giving, above all, is her focus in God's kingdom. I responded, "I am His mouthpiece." I had never said those words aloud before. The Holy Spirit imparts information into my mind and into my heart. The words that are so often confusing in the Bible suddenly have clarity, illuminating from the pages. Discernment is not a sufficient description. The revelation is in how He wants me to use the information. It's what He tells me to say to His people. It's in the way the Holy Spirit allows me to see people just before He crafts a message to deliver to them. It's in the glory of standing in front of a person wrapped in flesh but only seeing the part of them that they have yet to meet. I shared with Dr. Enola that I was not pursuing a ministry role. Instead, I was responding to the call.

The Lord sought me. He removed me from my comfy, cozy environment and positioned me in a cold, dark, sunken place. When He returned, He asked, "Tilicia, are you still there?" I replied, "Yes, Lord, I'm still here." I now personally understand the lesson God taught the Israelites when He brought them out of the wilderness. I just needed to *test you in order to know what was in your heart, whether or not you would keep his commands.* Could I have the heart of a servant in my darkest times? Coming out of the pit reminded me of Jesus' conversation with the Apostle Peter. Jesus said to Peter, "Feed my sheep." I went into the pit as a student, but I arose from the pit as a teacher. The Holy Spirit is my guide and my mentor. Like any good mentee, after spending quiet, personal time with my mentor, He now knows my heart, and I know His. Now, I can share all that He has taught me and all that He is teaching me.

"Give us this day, our daily bread." This is my favorite part of the Lord's prayer. I have always thought that the Lord gives us just enough to know that we are not moving forward in our strength and that we must come back to Him each and every day. This is just one layer of meaning. What if the Lord one day asked, "What did you do with the bread I gave to you yesterday? To say that I ate that bread seems insufficient. It is not using the bread He gives me each day. I'd like to say, "Lord, I returned a tenth of that bread, and with the rest, I fed your sheep. I fed your sheep plenty, knowing that I could come back to you each day, not for myself, but so I can continue to feed them." The Bible says, give and it will be given unto you exceedingly and abundantly (Ephesians 3:20). I give so that I may return to my heavenly Father for more, with full confidence that He knows how I will use it.

Chapter 11: (Conclusion) — Follow His Gifts To Your Bridegroom

²⁷ To this John replied, A person can receive only what is given them from heaven. ²⁸ You yourselves can testify that I said, "I am not the Messiah but am sent ahead of him. ²⁹ The bride belongs to the bridegroom. John 3:27-29

The relationship between Isaac and Rebekah can be used as a metaphor for the role of the Holy Spirit in our lives. When I was first introduced to this story, I did not value its importance in illustrating our intimacy with the Holy Spirit. But behind this story is a great revelation about the role of the Holy Spirit in bringing us to meet our bridegroom. For me, this story symbolizes the very essence of spiritual gifts as an invitation from our Heavenly Father. The servant was sent with gifts to get Rebekah (the bride) for Isaac (the bridegroom). Rebekah chooses to accept the invitation. After Rebekah accepts the invitation, it is the servant's responsibility to bring her to Isaac. In doing so, the servant is present with Rebekah for the entire journey to meet Isaac. When they were near,

Rebekah prepared herself for presentation to her bridegroom.

It's important for us to understand the perspectives of both the servant and Rebekah. Rebekah is being asked to trust the servant and his invitation. She is being asked to believe that the invitation is real. Then, there is the perspective of the servant. He comes to Rebekah bearing gifts for her and her family, and brings Rebekah to her bridegroom. I can imagine the servant's excitement. He has been tasked with an important mission. If the answer is "no," I can only imagine the devastation the servant would feel to have to return to his master empty-handed. Abraham tells his servant, 'If the woman does not accept the invitation, move on." Such is the case for the Holy Spirit, who comes bearing spiritual gifts and to bring us to our bridegroom. He comes with the hope that He does not have to move on.

There is excitement and anticipation at the opportunity to invite us to accept these gifts from the Spirit and bring us to our bridegroom. If the answer is "no," I could all but feel the despair. It brings the Holy Spirit joy to bring the invitation and to come bearing gifts that will reveal who we are in Christ. His revelation is that we were chosen. Similar to Rebekah, we were chosen for our willingness to serve. The challenge is that we must accept the invitation immediately because He has to return. The invitation is only available to us if we choose to accept it. But we must not tarry in making that choice.

The Holy Spirit was sent not *to* us but *for* us. When the Holy Spirit comes for us, He brings the spiritual gifts to help us learn more about our bridegroom as we draw nigh to Him. When we first receive the gifts, we place a high value on them. Receiving the gifts is a big deal. They help us to understand, they edify us, but ultimately, it's not about the gifts. When I received the invitation from the Holy Spirit, my focus was on the spiritual gifts because they were new to me. The gifts were needed to help me understand that the invitation was real, just as Rebekah needed her gifts to validate the invitation from her bridegroom. But I don't want you to miss the point. The gifts were brought to me to inform me that my bridegroom had called for me. I was chosen.

Like Rebekah, the decision to accept the call can be frightening, and the journey to our bridegroom may be a slow, lengthy process. In fact, similar to her journey through the desert, it will be bumpy, and you may want to stop or turn around. But the Holy Spirit will be there through the entire journey. What strikes me is that when Rebekah's family finds out that Abraham has sent for a bridegroom for Isaac, the family is excited, but they want Rebekah to wait before she leaves. The servant, however, says no, that they must not delay. Let me remind you that Rebekah is only eligible to receive the invitation because she is a part of Abraham's family (Galatians 3:29), but the reason she is CHOSEN is because she served the (Abraham's) servant. When we are called, we must make the decision Rebekah made. We must accept the invitation, and we must do it without haste. Don't allow His Holy Spirit to move on without you. Take the journey by way of the Holy Spirit to our bridegroom, who is our Heavenly Father.

Embrace and keep moving forward.

[13] ...When you believed, you were marked in him with a seal, the promised Holy Spirit, [14] who is a deposit guaranteeing our inheritance until the redemption of those who are God's possession—to the praise of his glory (Ephesians 1:13-14, NIV).

In the family of charismatic brothers and sisters in Christ who have received an invitation from the Holy Spirit to dwell within them, operating in the power of the Spirit may seem so common and simple. Yet, for those who are new to spiritual gifts, the experience of a working power that many believe should feel comforting can actually be a frightening or uncomfortable process, especially if you have never known that they exist. For those who are afraid of His manifesting power, let go and let God have His way. I pray that you do not allow fear or doubt to get the best of you. In John 14:11, Jesus tells his disciples, *"At least believe in the evidence of the works themselves. [12] Very truly, I tell you, whoever believes in me will do the works I have been doing, and they will do even greater things than these...*" When the Holy Spirit invites you to receive His spiritual gifts, I urge you to be of service and accept that you have been chosen by our Lord and Savior, Jesus Christ. It is a humbling experience to submit freely to the Holy Spirit to show Him that He can use you.

Today, I can freely say that my fears are not of God using me or even how He will use me. I have come to a place where I can be obedient when called upon by the Holy Spirit. My fears today are of what the Holy Spirit will reveal to me and what He will show me. Job said, *"I had heard of you by the hearing of the ear, but now my eye sees you."* (Job 42:5, ESV). Through the Holy Spirit, my spiritual eyes see the things that I could not have imagined in this physical world. The unveiling is a gift, an invitation that does not last long and does not remain with those who do not appreciate His gifts or are unwilling to be used to further His plans. Now is not a time for fear or resistance. This is a time for you to embrace all that the Holy Spirit is calling you to and all that awaits you. It's a time to move forward in faith, confidently knowing that He has already gone ahead of you and accept the invitation so that you, too, may be of service in His Holy Kingdom. *It is my sincere prayer that this book blesses you the way the Lord has blessed me. Many blessings to you!*

When The Holy Spirit Calls

[10]Therefore, my brothers and sisters, make every effort to confirm your calling and election. For if you do these things, you will never stumble, [11]and you will receive a rich welcome into the eternal kingdom of our Lord and Savior Jesus Christ.
(2 Peter 1:10-11, NIV)

Notes

Goll, J. (2017). The Discerner: Hearing, Confirming, and Acting on Prophetic Revelation. Whitaker House. New Kensington, PA.

Pickett, F. (2003). God's Purpose for You: Answer life's five key questions, Charisma House. Lake Mary, FL, p. 114.

Pickett, F. (2004). Walking in the Anointing of the Holy Spirit, Charisma House. Lake Mary, FL.